HAUNTED
DUNDEE

HAUNTED
DUNDEE

Geoff Holder

Acknowledgements

LIBRARIANS are authors' guardian angels, and I would like to express my profound thanks to the staff of the local studies sections of the A.K. Bell Library in Perth and the Wellgate Library in Dundee, and further thanks for permission to reproduce various historic images. For assistance, co-operation and for answering my pesky questions, my gratitude goes out to: Lisa Douglas, Debbie Rooney, Kevin Connolly and Mary Archibald at Verdant Works; Dundee Heritage Trust; South Georgia Heritage Trust; Bob Hovell, Ship Manager, HMS *Unicorn*; playwright Kevin Dyer and theatre director Michael Judge; tour guide Anthony Cox (www.taysidehistoricaltours.com); Murdo Wilson at Claypotts Castle; and Marek at Dundee Backpackers Hostel.

I am especially grateful to all those who shared their personal stories with me, including: June Kelso; Colin McLeod; Sarah Fraser (with extra gratitude for granting permission to reproduce her sketch); and Victor and Elena Peterson of Mains Castle. None of their stories have previously been published. The Ghost Club investigation, led by Derek Green, gave me the opportunity to explore RRS *Discovery* under unusual circumstances. Ségolène Dupuy did wonders on the photographs and Jenni Wilson drew the maps.

This book is a companion to the author's *Paranormal Dundee* (2010) and is part of a series of works by Geoff Holder dedicated to the mysterious and paranormal. For more information, or to contribute your own experience, please visit www.geoffholder.com. And say hello to webmaster Jamie Cook while you're there.

To Shade and Slick – companions both. Now go and lie down and let me work!

First published 2012

The History Press
The Mill, Brimscombe Port
Stroud, Gloucestershire, GL5 2QG
www.thehistorypress.co.uk

© Geoff Holder, 2012

The right of Geoff Holder to be identified as the Author
of this work has been asserted in accordance with the
Copyrights, Designs and Patents Act 1988.

British Library Cataloguing in Publication Data.
A catalogue record for this book is available from the British Library.

ISBN 978 0 7524 5849 6
Typesetting and origination by The History Press
Printed in Great Britain

Contents

Places to Visit   7

Introduction   8

one   The White Ladies   11

two   Contemporary Encounters with the Supernatural   28

three   Malevolent Entities   38

four   The Den o'Mains   46

five   Spooky Ships – *Discovery* and the Frigate *Unicorn*   55

six   Fakes, Frauds & Folklore – and Spring-Heeled Jack!   63

seven   'Traditional' Ghosts   74

eight   Historic Hauntings   87

Bibliography   93

Index   96

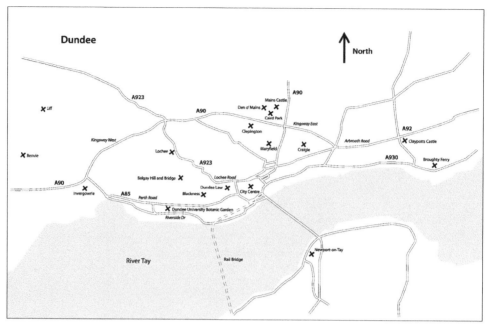

Dundee

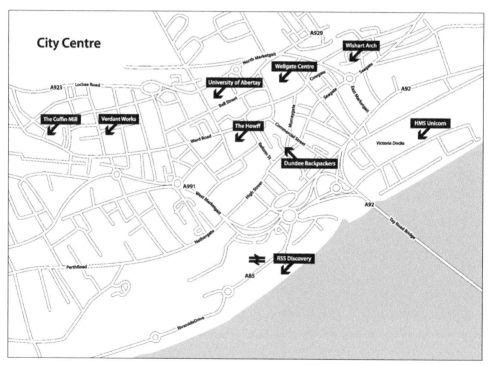

Dundee

Places to Visit

The following locations are open to visitors:

Claypotts Castle/Castle Gardens: Claypotts Road, DD5 3JY. View exterior only. To visit interior, call 01786 431324 in advance. Admission free. No internal wheelchair access.

Discovery Point Visitor Centre: Discovery Quay, DD1 4XA. Tel: 01382 309060. www.rrsdiscovery.com. Open Monday–Saturday 10 a.m.–6 p.m. (Sun 11 a.m.) from April to October; 10 a.m.–5 p.m. rest of year (Sunday 11 a.m.). Admission charge. Wheelchair access throughout museum and to main deck of the historic ship only.

Dundee Backpackers: 71 High Street, DD1 1SD. Tel: 01382 224 646. Public access (including wheelchair access) to display area in inner courtyard only. Admission free.

The Frigate *Unicorn*, Victoria Dock: DD1 3BP. Tel: 01382 200900. www.frigateunicorn.org/. Open 10 a.m.–5 p.m. all week from April to October; November to March: 12 p.m.–4 p.m. Wednesday, Thursday and Friday, and 10 a.m.–4 p.m. Saturday and Sunday. Admission charge. Wheelchair access to Gun Deck only.

Verdant Works: West Henderson's Wynd, DD1 5BT. Tel: 01382 309060. www.rrsdiscovery.com. Open Monday–Saturday 10 a.m.–6 p.m. (Sun 11 a.m.) from April to October; 10 a.m.–5 p.m. Wednesday-Saturday rest of year (Sunday 11 a.m.). Admission charge. Wheelchair access throughout museum (note courtyard is cobbled).

Mains Castle welcomes enquiries for weddings and corporate events: www.mainscastle.com. The castle is not open to the general public.

Many of the other locations mentioned in this book are private; please respect the privacy of the residents.

Introduction

ON my shelves are two classics from an earlier generation of ghost books: *The Ghost Hunter's Road Book* by John Harries, which came out in 1968 and has more than 400 entries across Britain, and *Haunted Britain* by Anthony D. Hippisley Coxe, published in 1973 with over 1,000 entries covering England, Wales, Scotland and the Isle of Man.

Dundee is not mentioned in either of them.

Neither does Dundee feature in more modern supernatural surveys, such as *The Ghost Tour of Great Britain: Scotland* by Richard Felix (2006), Roddy Martine's *Supernatural Scotland* (2003) and *Haunted Scotland* (2010), the huge Readers' Digest work *The Most Amazing Haunted & Mysterious Places in Britain* (2009), and Derek Acorah's *Haunted Britain* (2006). As far as ghost-hunters are concerned, it appears that Dundee is not even on the map.

But, as the man said, it ain't necessarily so, and Dundee has been unjustly ignored. In this book you hold in your hand, this oversight will be corrected. We are about to explore several centuries of Dundonian hauntings. Here you'll find stories of poltergeists, malevolent entities, apparitions, strange sounds, doppelgängers, visionary experiences and much more. The incidents range from 1706 to the present day. There is also, you should be warned, a wholesale demolition of some of the city's best-loved traditional spectres. And you will find a full stock of fakelore and frauds, for the tendency to hoax the supernatural is always with us. In 2011, for example, there was an attempt in the local press to suggest that a particular stone in the old graveyard of the Howff was a memorial to Grissel Jaffray, who was executed for witchcraft in 1669. I covered Grissel's trial extensively in my previous book *Paranormal Dundee*, and it is quite evident that the 'memorial' episode is not just bad history, but a naked attempt to foist a fake story onto the public. Beware of false paranormalists, my friends.

Other than those stories personally related to me, the episodes in *Haunted Dundee* were taken from a variety of published sources, such as books, academic journals and websites, all of which are credited in the text. The bibliography allows anyone interested to go to the original sources and see if they agree with my interpretation. Many of the older stories in this book have not seen the light of day for well over a century, and most were found in old newspapers. Dundee's two principal papers have a confusing history. The *Dundee Weekly*

A postcard of a typical Dundee scene from 1905. (Author's collection)

Dundee High Street in 1906. Many of the buildings shown have since vanished. (Author's collection)

Advertiser which launched in 1801, later beame the *Dundee, Perth & Cupar Advertiser* and finally the plain *Dundee Advertiser* from 1861. The *Dundee Courier* commenced publication in 1817 and, at various times in its history, was known as the *Constitutional Dundee Courier*, the *Dundee Courier & Daily Argus*, the *Dundee Courier & Argus*, and the *Dundee Courier & Argus and Northern Warder*. In 1926 both papers merged to form the *Courier & Advertiser*. To keep matters simple I have used the single names *Advertiser* and *Courier* for the older editions, and the title *Courier & Advertiser* for all stories after 1926.

Up until the seventeenth century, Dundee was Scotland's second city after Edinburgh, a dynamic and prosperous seaport with trading links across northern Europe. In the late 1700s, the economic focus turned to industry, primarily textile production. Soon dozens of mills were processing flax brought from the Baltic. The population doubled, then doubled again, then rose exponentially as people flocked in from the countryside. From the 1850s, the dominant industry was jute production, a coarse but versatile fibre imported from India. Dundee became a city almost exclusively devoted to textile manufacturing. Jute spinning and weaving employed 40,000 workers across 125 mills, while linen production continued to employ thousands more. A forest of 200 tall chimneys greeted visitors, with a dense ring of industry encircling the city centre and docks. In a (successful) effort to keep wages down, exploitative employers favoured women and children as mill workers. Working-class housing and living conditions were appalling, and Dundee became something of a classic Victorian sinkhole. In the twentieth century, jute went into terminal decline, and in the post-war years the city has struggled with the effects of post-industrial collapse and urban decay.

Despite all this, the medieval and Renaissance hodgepodge of the city centre remained largely intact until 1871, and, if circumstances had been different, Dundee would have been an architectural gem today, on a par with Edinburgh's Old Town. But a combination of political infighting, financial problems and disastrous planning decisions has swept away the vast majority of Dundee's historic buildings. As will be clear from the cases studied here, this has had a profound impact on what might be termed the city's haunted heritage.

Welcome to Haunted Dundee. It's back on the map.

We folks wha occupy these coasts
And pride oursel's on our discernin',
Are no gien to belief in ghosts
They tally not wi' our book-learnin';

Wraiths, warlocks, bogles, how we jeer them
And yet, in truth, the maist o's fear them!

'The White Lady of Claypotts Castle' – Joseph Lee

one

The White Ladies

BRITISH 'ghost-lore' is dominated by certain kinds of female apparitions. There are endless Green Ladies and Grey Ladies, with slightly fewer Pink Ladies – all named for the period costume they are usually seen wearing. White Ladies are also populous, and Dundee has at least four examples.

The White Lady O' Balgay Bridge

Q: Do you feel safe in your area?

A: I do feel quite safe in my area. Your [*sic*] fine as long as you avoid the cemetery at nights so you a) don't get scared by the mysterious souls that skulk around the graves and b) don't get eaten alive by the ghost that patrols the white lady bridge.

This was one of the responses to the 'You & Your Area' survey conducted by Young Scot Dundee from September to December 2006, and held online at www.youngscot. org/dundee and www.dundeecity.gov.uk. Over 500 eleven to fifteen year olds took part. Most responded to the question regarding safety by mentioning concerns over gangs, junkies, drunks, graffiti and other urban problems. This particular pupil, however, concentrated specifically on the terrors of the White Lady of Balgay Bridge.

Balgay Bridge is the cast-iron Victorian footway that stretches high over the ravine of the Windy Glack, connecting the recreational woodlands of Balgay Hill to the east with the tree-lined footpaths of Balgay Cemetery further west. Widely known among the residents of the Lochee area, and a favourite childhood spook, the White Lady features in a number of different stories:

She is seen reading a letter then bursting into tears before disappearing – or jumping off the bridge.
She runs from the bridge into the cemetery, weeping.
She can be summoned at midnight by walking across the bridge three (or five, or seven) times.
She can turn those who unwittingly summon her into a pool of blood.
She can eat people alive (*see* above).
She can push unsuspecting bystanders off the bridge.

Balgay Park in 1907. Note Balgay Bridge in the background. (Author's collection)

Balgay Bridge today, taken from the Windy Glack. (The Author)

She is heard screaming at midnight as she plunges to her death.

She is rarely seen, but her crying and footsteps are often heard, and dogs grow nervous at her invisible presence.

Wonderfully evocative stuff, I'm sure you'll agree, combining traditional elements of the ghost story with aspects that are distinctly demonic (and with a clear hint of Clive Barker's *Candyman*). There is just one problem with this rich skein of supernaturalism – there are no reliable accounts for any of it. Stories there are in abundance; sightings, however, are conspicuous through their absence. The White Lady exists in a web of rumour, thrice-told-tales, anecdote, 'foaftale' (friend-of-a-friend tale), childhood recollections and urban legend. In other words, she is a folk ghost.

What follows is a tentative exploration of the factors that may have contributed to this folkloric phantom. As with most areas of the paranormal, it is difficult – not to say foolhardy – to make definitive pronouncements about the absolute black-and-white reality or unreality of specific phenomena. However, given that (a) the White Lady is widely-known and (b) there are no dependable reports, we are entitled to interrogate the context of the haunting to see if anything useful comes out of the combination of analysis and speculation.

The first place to start is the physical environment. The bridge at Balgay stretches for 80ft over the ravine. Crafted out of decorative cast-iron, and recently attractively repainted, it is a striking structure both geographically and aesthetically, and could be said to be in contrast with its immediate setting. To the east is the hill of Balgay Park, a popular recreational area at the centre of Lochee's green lung, with Lochee Park and Victoria Park stretching contigu-

ously to the north and south respectively. The space was purchased as a public area by the council in 1869, being carved out of the former Balgay Estate. From the very first it was designed as a People's Park: a working-class recreational area where the half-life of industrial squalor could be temporarily forgotten. A plaque on the bridge states: BALGAY HILL RECREATION GROUNDS PROVIDED BY THE COMMUNITY OF DUNDEE FOR THE USE OF THE PEOPLE, AND OPENED 20 SEPTEMBER 1871. Balgay Cemetery (formerly known as the Western Necropolis) is on the opposite side of the ravine, with the older (late-Victorian) monuments in the north part, close to the bridge. In *The Municipal History of the Royal Burgh of Dundee*, published in 1873, J.M. Beatts gives his thoughts on the aesthetics of this attractive wooded cemetery:

An hour's retirement and contemplation in the precincts of these beautiful grounds cannot fail to impress the mind with the idea that both nature and art have combined to render the place most fitting for reflection on the power of the Creator, the shortness of human life, the immortality of the soul, and the heavenly rest

Another view of Balgay Bridge. The entrance to Balgay Cemetery can be seen in the background. (The Author)

13

beyond the grave prepared for the people of God.

The ravine of the Windy Glack always divided Balgay, and so the bridge was built to provide ease of access between the two parts of the hill. From one point of view then, the bridge is a link between the lands of the living and the dead. Such transition places are liminal places, psycho-geographical hotspots where supernatural episodes – or at least stories of supernatural episodes – tend to be concentrated. Liminality, the notion of crossing borders (such as between the mundane world and the netherworld, or between one state and another) is a key concept in magic and myth. Midnight, the moment between one day and another, is a liminal time; ten to eleven is not. Bogs and caves are liminal places, as are parish boundaries, doors, gates, churchyard walls, seashores, tunnels and thresholds. Balgay Bridge is definitely liminal.

It is, of course, also very high, towering 80ft above the (now-paved) ravine below. There is something about such an expanse that, in a small number of people, fosters thoughts of jumping into the void below. The Glack, and the Balgay area in general, had a questionable reputation up until the early nineteenth century, and there are numerous newspaper reports of footpads, smugglers, and assaults on women.

Balgay, then, was a place with a pre-existing reputation for dark deeds. Its physical setting, a ravine between two hills crossed by a strikingly designed bridge, is impressive and unusual. Part of the bridge leads directly to a cemetery. Since becoming a park the area is both popular and, because of the woodland, secluded. And there is a question of whether the massive iron structure of the bridge somehow channels or deflects an electromagnetic field – and EM fields are known to have an impact on human cognition, including influencing perceptions of apparent supernatural events. All these factors contribute to a sense that Balgay Bridge is psycho-geographically potent; a place where things can happen.

That, in itself, may not be enough to generate a haunting. Balgay, however, also has a known history of tragedy and violent death, all grist for the mythic mill.

Only one accidental death is on record. On 21 March 1846, the *Scotsman* reported that a blacksmith, James Ferrand, had been killed by a landslide at Hillside Quarry on Balgay Hill – but the area soon had its fair share of suicide attempts (and, you will recall, the White Lady is, at least according to some versions, supposed to throw herself off the bridge). The first recorded suicide on the hill was that of George Bruce, a weaver from Henderson's Wynd, who was reported in the *Advertiser* as being found dead on the morning of 6 September 1837. On 15 May 1883, the *Scotsman* reported that the previous day, a drunken woman named Bridget Finney, or Finnie, had attempted to jump from the bridge; her death was only prevented by a groundsman named Hugh Smith who, being deaf and mute, could not call for help, and had to hang on to the thrashing woman until others spotted the struggle and rushed to assist. Four days later, the *Weekly News* reported that, 'the woman Bridget Finnie or Mullare … was called in to answer to a charge of drunkenness ... She had been liberated on a bail of 5s, and, failing to answer to her name, the pledge was forfeited.' Two years on, twenty-eight-year-old James Newlands blew his brains out with a single shot to his temple (the report was in the *Courier* on 30 January 1885); in 1894, thirty-seven-year-old William Jarvis Parker sat on his family burying-place in the cemetery and put two bullets in his head

Is this where the White Lady patrols? (The Author)

One of the Victorian gravestones in Balgay Cemetery. (The Author)

(*Courier*, 24 September); and finally, fifty-two-year-old Roland Smith threw himself off the bridge in 1898 (*Courier*, 27 June).

But none of these tragedies provide us with a link to the White Lady, who, according to the standard tale, was both determined to die and determinedly female. There are, however, two possible candidates for the source of the legend: Janet Fenton and Christina Fraser.

Janet Fenton's demise was reported in the *Scotsman* on 10 November 1882:

> Yesterday morning a widow named Fenton committed suicide by throwing herself over a suspension bridge in Balgay Public Park, Dundee. She fell a distance of 30 feet and was killed on the spot, her body being terribly mangled. The woman's mind was affected since the loss of her husband, a mechanic, who was scalded to death in a Dundee millpond several years ago.

Logie resident Janet was fifty-nine years old, and left behind seven children. The *Courier*, for 15 January 1875, described how her husband, James Steel, had suffered an appalling death after falling into a hot-water tank at the South Dudhope Works.

As for Christina Fraser, her sad death appeared in the *Advertiser* on Wednesday, 17 May 1911:

> The woman who fell from the bridge in Balgay Park on Friday succumbed to her injuries yesterday in Dundee Royal Infirmary. Two boys, cycling through the park shortly after six o'clock in the evening were startled to see a woman hanging from the high bridge. Before they could reach the bridge to render assistance the woman relaxed her grip, falling

to the steep bank below and rolling onto the path. When picked up she was still alive but unconscious, and was removed to the Infirmary, where she was identified as Christina Fraser (53), millworker, who resided with her brother and sister at 69 Ure Street. Her injuries were of a serious nature, but she lingered until yesterday.

The *Scotsman* for the same day added another detail:

> Recently the bridge was securely fenced because of the number of deaths connected with it, and how the woman managed to get on the outside is as yet unexplained.

So, White Lady-wise, this is what I suggest happened. The Balgay area had an existing reputation, compounded by a rake of tragedies and dramatic events, and further focused by the striking and at times eerie situation of the bridge. The location's locus as a suicide spot became the overarching narrative, with just the right *coup de grâce* provided by the awful deaths of Janet Fenton and Christina Fraser. Out of this rich stew of dark events and grim geography, the place garnered a 'no' canny' rep, and the White Lady was born. Perpetuated by generations of children, the ghost story became further elaborated and expanded, so that soon everyone knew it was 'true', simply because it was so widespread. Of course, I could be utterly mistaken, and the next time I stroll over the bridge a rather miffed spectre may come and give me a piece of her mind; but for my money the White Lady O' Balgay is a figment of the folk mind, a Lochee legend.

The White Lady of the Coffin Mill

> Hundreds of people gathered in Lower Pleasance last night when it was reported a ghost called 'The White Lady' appeared...

Such was the opening line of an article in the *Courier & Advertiser* on 5 September 1945, headlined: 'GHOST WALKS BRIDGE – DUNDEE THRONG VISITS SCENE – "THE WHITE LADY" OF COFFIN MILL.' According to an unnamed elderly woman who was interviewed by the newspaper, the phantom was the spirit of a mill girl who died when her long hair became trapped in a loom and she was crushed to death. Again according to this anonymous local witness, the accident had occurred in the first week of September 'seventy years ago' – and the ghost periodically returned, pacing the enclosed exterior bridge that connected two parts of the mill. So large were the numbers gathered, that at 10 p.m. that the police arrived and told the crowd to disperse. Some did so, but many hung around the adjacent Brook Street in the hope of seeing the ghost. The article went on to say that:

> To satisfy the public that everything was normal, a police officer had a street lamp lit at the junction, which resulted in the crowd going from Brook Street into Lower Pleasance. Many of the younger folk in the crowd began throwing stones at the windows, causing a lot of damage. The street was littered with broken glass, and for some unaccountable reason other people broke milk bottles on the causeway at the entrance to the mill. To fully satisfy the crowd there was no ghost, a police officer, accompanied by the works

The Coffin Mill, with the White Lady's bridge. (The Author)

watchman, made a tour of the building shining their torches over every window as they went.

What with a large, unruly crowd, a police presence, and stone-throwing and glass-breaking, this sounds like a near-riot – and all because of a rumour of the return of the White Lady of Coffin Mill.

The Coffin Mill was the south range of Logie Works, Dundee's first really big textiles factory. It was built in 1828 but was much expanded in later years, becoming the largest flax works of the nineteenth century, from 1842 to 1865, and employing 2,500 workers at its height. Still there, but now converted to flats, the mill occupies a quadrangle of land bounded by Brook Street, Brewery Lane, Lower Pleasance and Horsewater Wynd, halfway between Lochee Road and Blackness Road – at the heart of what had been a dense industrial forest of tall chimneys. Most are now gone, their associated works demolished or converted to other purposes. No one really knows who gave the building its name of the Coffin Mill; the usual explanation is that it derives from the coffin-shaped interior courtyard, enclosed within three

A view of the bridge from within the former mill's coffin-shaped courtyard. (The Author)

forbiddingly tall ranges and open to the south-east – the end at which a cast-iron bridge crosses from one range to the other.

The mill, owned by A. & D. Edward, closed it doors in 1876, no bidder having been found for the £67,000 asking price. From 1880 onwards, Logie Works was partitioned into smaller units, and the Coffin Mill became a jute-spinning operation, going on to change hands (and function) several times. In 1945, when the near-riot occurred, the premises were owned by Fisher Gillis & Co., wholesale cabinet makers.

The Coffin Mill had its fair share of dark deeds. In 1828, a workman died during the erection of the chimney. On 4 August 1864, the *Scotsman* announced that a young boy named John Wighton had lost his life while effectively joyriding on the works' elevator. Concerned that he and his companion would be discovered, he was keeping watch over the lip of the elevator. 'While in this position,' the paper sadly noted, 'he was crushed between the ascending box and one of the floors.' You would think that either of these two accidents would provide sufficient horror to kick-start a ghostly legend, but the Coffin Mill remained resolutely untroubled by the shades of broken chimney-wrights or decapitated children. Instead, it became home, so the story has it, to the White Lady.

The most common origin of the ghost is that which is described in the report on the previous page – her long hair became entangled in the machinery and she was killed. A search of newspapers from the nineteenth and early twentieth century reveals no record of such an accident. Of course, this did not mean it did not take place – simply that it was not recorded, seemingly. In a variant of the legend, she is said to have run out onto the bridge after the accident and, blinded by pain, fell fatally onto the cobbles below. In a recent post on a Dundee chat room, a contributor claimed that the ghost was headless (presumably having been rendered this way by the accident). And thus the story continues to mutate and grow.

In the mid-twentieth century, everyone in the area knew the story of the White Lady of Coffin Mill. She was a famous ghost, her tale passed on from generation to generation, becoming part of the folklore of both place (Blackness) and time (childhood). And along with her fame, she shared another attribute with the White Lady O' Balgay – there were no reliable sightings of her.

Of course, people may have indeed seen the spectre, but if they did, none of these reports made it to the newspapers, or into books, or were published in any other form. The White Lady was a fully believed-in rumour, but a rumour nonetheless. Like her Balgay counterpart, she was a folk ghost.

Or was she? Because there is another possibility – that the White Lady was genuinely spotted, but not in the Coffin Mill; she may have been seen in an altogether different industrial concern, the Verdant Works.

The White Lady of the Verdant Works

Verdant Works on West Henderson Wynd has been both a flax and a jute mill. After the decline in the jute industry the mill went through several owners, and was used for a variety of trades in the twentieth century, including the large-scale recycling of jute waste, the curing of rabbit skins for the fashion trade, and scrap-metal dealing. The derelict building was rescued in 1991 by the Dundee Heritage Trust, and is now an award-winning museum, dedicated to the industrial history of the city, with working power looms and other manufacturing machinery. It is a fascinating visit.

In around 1953, when he was about five or six years old, Kevin Connolly, the present museum caretaker, remembers being regularly taken by his grandmother from his tenement to a nearby washhouse. In conversation, Mr Connolly has a vivid recollection of his early life in the Blackness area. The route took them past

Verdant Works industrial museum. (The Author)

19

The bridge on which the White Lady was seen. (The Author)

On the bridge, looking towards the east and south ranges. (The Author)

Verdant Works, and he clearly recalls her telling him that the White Lady walked across the bridge that connects two parts of the complex, which is clearly visible from the gateway entrance. So, in contrast with many other local people, Kevin Connolly grew up with the belief that the White Lady haunted not the Coffin Mill but Verdant Works.

An interesting coincidence? Or is it the same ghost? It is common for ghosts, in this type of story, to flit between different locations; they do not have a fixed haunting site. But then, during the summer of 2007 or 2008, Mr Connolly was working late at the museum, painting the café while his seven-year-old daughter Louise looked on. As he stood in the courtyard locking the café door at 9 p.m., with a bright clear sky behind him, Louise looked around and said, 'Who's that lady, Daddy?' The care-

taker turned to where she was pointing but saw nothing. When he asked his daughter whom she was talking about, she said she had seen a 'lovely lady'. She was dressed all in white and had long, blonde hair; the girl saw her walking across the bridge from left to right (north to south).

Could the original sightings of the White Lady have taken place at Verdant Works and somehow been confusingly transferred to the Coffin Mill? Although the two mills are hardly adjacent – the former is some 500 yards east of the latter – and the Coffin Mill is far larger, they do share some physical similarities. In particular, both have a bridge overlooking the inner courtyard. Verdant Works commenced in 1833, being gradually expanded piecemeal until 1870, when 500 workers were employed. As a result of this slightly irregular growth, it was found necessary to erect an open-air walkway to connect

The view from the bridge. The lower door (No. 2) is at the end of the corridor. A ghostly voice was heard here. (The Author)

the north and east ranges. Unlike the Coffin Mill equivalent, the Verdant Works' bridge is not particularly striking, being short, on the first floor, bounded on one side by a wall, and not freestanding, as it runs above a ground-floor structure. At the Coffin Mill, by contrast, the freestanding bridge is much higher, much longer, much more obvious, and much more dramatic (and bears a distinctive resemblance to the Bridge of Balgay). If the Verdant Works' bridge is indeed the locus, could the story have been transferred to the Coffin Mill simply through people confusing two mills with external bridges, and plumping for the more impressive one? I have no idea whether this is the case, but there are other elements that give weight to Verdant Works' claim.

For a start, we have what many a good ghost story needs, an 'origin death'. Two people are known to have died in Verdant Works. The *Advertiser* for Friday, 4 March 1853, had the following announcement:

> We regret to record the death of James Clark, a worker at the Verdant Mill, which took place on Wednesday evening, in consequence of an accident which happened to him while attending to his employment on the previous day. It appears he was caught by a belt of the machinery, which carried him rapidly to the roof of the building, where he was three times revolved round one of the shafts before he could be extricated. He was conveyed to the Infirmary as soon as possible, but the poor fellow was so much bruised that death was the result.

But perhaps more germane to our search for a female figure is the brief report in the same paper for Friday, 26 March 1852:

The corridor to the Verdant Works' archives, where many staff feel uneasy. (The Author)

John McKenna, who held the caretaker's post before Kevin Connolly. He told the paper about being called out several times by the police, who were convinced that the place had been hit by burglars or vandals. Lights were on, and loud sounds as if of machinery were heard. On each occasion there was no break-in and no machinery was running (Kevin Connolly had similar experiences in the early 2000s). There were several other phenomena from the 1990s, 'When the workshop suddenly became chillingly cold,' said Mr McKenna …

> I would look for an open window or some other explanation but could never find one. The most fearful experience is the workshop door. Several moments after it closes and without the door moving, you hear the sound of it closing again.

Then there was the relocation of objects:

> It moves things that you've laid down behind you, but at least it doesn't throw them around the place. I used to blame the forgetfulness of old age when I couldn't find things I'd laid down but it happens to other people too.

On Tuesday afternoon a girl, employed in Verdant Mill, got entangled about a carding machine, and sustained such injuries before she could be released as to occasion instantaneous death.

No details are given for the girl, and so we do not know her age or even her name. Could this anonymous victim of an atrocious industrial accident be the source of the 'origin death' for the legend of the White Lady? Once again, I can make no claims one way or another – but in terms of unusual phenomena, Verdant Works is hardly dormant.

On 27 December 1999, the *Daily Record* ran a story on the hauntings in the museum, with a number of quotes from

The caretaker, a former mechanical engineer in a jute mill, seemed to have come round to thinking he was not alone in the mill at night:

> Trust me, when you're wandering round the pitch black corners of a deserted mill at midnight, you really don't need to believe in ghosts … [but] despite my previous doubts about the existence of ghosts, I have to admit I get a strong feeling someone else is there.

My own enquiries elicited additional details. Around the start of 2008, the last

Verdant Works. The door on the first-floor landing, where a reflected apparition was seen. (The Author)

We can, of course, suspect that faulty wiring or some other mundane issue could be the source of at least some of these incidents, and pigeons are known to inhabit the echoey semi-derelict part of the old mill, so odd sounds could have a prosaic origin. Furthermore, the physical setting – large open spaces with pools of shadow, a network of dark corridors and access areas, and a centuries-old building that creaks with the weather – is certainly conducive to what might be termed an 'environment of anxiety'; exactly the kind of place where it is easy to convince yourself that you are not alone, and that your unwanted companions are not entirely flesh and blood…

But, on the other hand, can such environmental and psychological issues really explain some of the reported phenomena – phenomena that, as we shall see, apparently encompass anomalous sounds, ghostly speech, and multiple apparitions?

In the summer of 2009, the previously empty first-floor offices above the café were taken over by the South Georgia Heritage Trust, an organisation dedicated to the protection of the sub-Antarctic island of South Georgia. In the months prior to the SGHT moving in, the rooms seemed to be the focus of low-level incidents. On several occasions Lisa Douglas, the supervisor at the museum, was working in the café first thing in the morning, when she heard the sound of a chair being dragged across the floor above. Typically this took place on weekend mornings, before the attraction opened for the day, and when the only other members of staff present were opening up the far end of the museum. So, not only was there no obvious human agency for the noises, but the offices were carpeted, while the sound was definitely of furniture being dragged across bare floorboards. Lisa has not heard any

person in the building, while locking up, would sometimes hear the internal telephone ringing, even though any external call would have had to come through the switchboard, which was always unstaffed at that time of day. In interviews, several members of staff have described the empty museum at night as being 'eerie', 'spooky' or 'scary'. Debbie Rooney, for example, who in June 2011 had only been working at the museum for six weeks, told me that she hated being alone among the exhibits on the first floor; she felt as if there was a sense of presence there, and was especially uncomfortable in the windowless corridor leading to the archives section. In contrast, RSS *Discovery*, the historic ship where she normally worked, seemed to her to have an entirely benign atmosphere (*see* Chapter five for more on *Discovery*, which is also allegedly haunted).

further noises since the SGHT arrived, but in 2011 her colleague, Debbie Rooney, was alone in the building early one morning when she heard footsteps in the unoccupied room above. In contrast, the staff of the South Georgia Heritage Trust, although aware of the alleged haunting, have not experienced any anomalous incidents.

At around 3.30 p.m. on a dark afternoon in the winter of 2009/2010, Lisa Douglas was cleaning the glass in the door leading to the SGHT offices when she saw a figure reflected in the left-hand pane. It was a small boy wearing a flat cap and a waistcoat. He was not looking at her but staring into space rather vacantly. Lisa looked behind her but there was no one in the short corridor, so she carried on working. Once again, she saw the boy's reflection, and once again, the space behind her was empty. After the third sighting she looked behind her into the empty corridor, and finished up; as she did so she heard footsteps going down the stairs.

The location for this unusual experience is a short landing on the first floor above the café. A lift opens here, and is used by members of the public who cannot manage the stairs. On either side of the lift are the stairs going down to the ground floor and up to the second floor. Directly opposite the glass-panelled door to the SGHT is a nondescript door with no decoration; it opens into an equally mundane L-shaped corridor that leads out onto the bridge and the first-floor exhibits in the east range. There is nothing on the landing or through any of the doors that could provide a source for the reflection, and Lisa was certain she was alone – indeed, the museum was almost certainly bereft of visitors that afternoon.

Up to this point the experiences were not alarming in any way, but Lisa found that this was to change. About 5.15 or 5.30 p.m. one day, early in 2011, Lisa was completing her supervisory lock-up in the ground-floor corridor, which runs along the south range leading to the fire exit and a large industrial door. Part of the original works, it is not an area to which the public has access, and there are no windows. The big door at the end was locked from the inside, and a small door opposite it leads nowhere. Basically, when all locked up there is only one door in and out of the rather chilly corridor, and that door is towards the eastern end. Having checked that the exterior door to the west was locked, Lisa moved to the furthest eastern recess and switched off a light. This, however, made the entire area pitch black, and so she turned it back on again and moved back a short distance to the access door, looking for a second off switch just to the left of the door. As she did so, a gruff male voice sounded from the far end of the corridor to her right, 'Don't turn off the light,' it growled. In the best traditions of such incidents, Lisa turned tail and fled.

On a sunny day in May 2011, Lisa and I attempted to recreate the incident. If the fire exit was indeed locked, there is no way that anyone could have entered or hidden in the western end of the corridor, the place where the voice came from. In addition, sightlines are clear, the walls are thick, and there is no view into the corridor from outside. With the light out, the corridor is almost entirely in deep darkness. As I stood at the east end of the corridor repeating the phrase, 'Don't turn off the light,' Lisa listened to the way my voice sounded as I changed position in the long, narrow space; it left her with the impression that when the original voice had spoken, it was moving along the corridor towards her.

In the most recent incident, at the start of May 2011, Lisa was locking up in the Social History Gallery on the first floor.

Once again, it was around 5.15 or 5.30 p.m. The area has a number of screens showing a variety of audio-visual programmes. When Lisa turned off all the electricity in the switch room, there was enough filtered daylight to see clearly, and she was certain that all the screens were off. Then, on the left-hand screen of a two-screen console, a woman appeared. She was slim, and wearing some form of headgear (or perhaps had her hair pulled back). In a clear Scottish accent, she said, 'Don't turn off the light.'

This was the second time Lisa ran away scared. A few weeks later, we attempted to replicate the environment. Even with the lights out, the exhibit area can be easily navigated in the diffused light of a May evening. The screen on which the woman appeared displays only images of old industrial scenes – there is nothing in the visuals or soundtrack of the AV display that could be mistaken for the woman Lisa described. One intriguing feature is that both incidents centred round the phrase 'Don't turn off the light', just as Lisa was indeed turning off lights. Also, the Social History Gallery on the first floor and the fire exit corridor on the ground floor are effectively one above the other, being connected by a staff-only staircase.

What does any of this mean? Is Verdant Works actually haunted? I honestly have no idea. Is there a connection to the supposed White Lady, which is where all this started? Once again, I am in the dark.

Verdant Works. The display in the Social History Gallery where an apparition was seen and heard. (The Author)

The White Lady of Benvie

This is our most elusive of the White Ladies, known only from a single reference, and with almost no confirmatory detail.

Only a fragment of ivy-cloaked wall and a postcard-sized graveyard remains of the church at the hamlet of Benvie, north of Invergowrie (National Grid Reference NO3282 3145). According to one of a series of articles in the *Courier,* entitled, 'Wanderings About the Antique Places & Churchyards of Forfarshire and Borders of Perthshire, &c.' (8 November 1848), a female spirit haunted the area in the sixteenth century. Each night she would walk up and down the banks of the stream in a white garment, to the alarm of the local people. Eventually the local clergyman, dressed in his robes and with his Bible in his hand, accosted the spirit and demanded, 'In the name of the Lord of Hosts, who art thou, and what dost thou want?' 'Holy man,' she replied:

I am the spirit of a victim of the plague, who, being a stranger here, my body was clandestinely buried in unconsecrated ground; remove it to the consecrated churchyard, and out of the spot where it has lain will spring forth water that will be an infallible cure for the plague in all future ages.

The last ivy-covered fragment of Benvie church. (The Author)

The minister duly agreed, and when the bones were re-interred in holy ground, the well proved to be a prophylactic against plague. The only other mention of the White Lady is almost forty years later, in Alex Warden's four-volume *Angus or Forfarshire of 1880-84*, which replicates the *Courier* piece almost word-for-word.

Benvie ceased to exist as a separate parish in 1758. By the 1790s, when the first Statistical Account of Scotland was compiled, the spring was still in existence, but was only visited by a small number of elderly supplicants seeking a general pick-me-up. By the time the second Statistical Account of the parish was written in 1842, the Medicine Well, as it was known, had fallen out of use.

The churchman who laid the ghost is not named, and it is not even clear if he was a pre-Reformation Catholic or a post-Reformation Protestant. No tradition ascribes any of the existing graves to the re-interred bones, and anyway the earliest slabs are seventeenth century and the graveyard was re-landscaped and built up in the early nineteenth century. The spring itself, which was found on the south bank of the Fowlis Burn, has been dry for at least thirty years. No existing or recent tradition of the White Lady of Benvie can be found, and her brief legend has entirely withered away.

two

Contemporary Encounters with the Supernatural

Freedom of Information> Disclosure Log Please could you give me details (of) reports of UFOs, ghosts, witches, vampires and zombies received by the force in the last 3 calendar years. Q1 – The date/time/location of report. Q2 – Brief details of the report, i.e. a bright red light in the sky; a ghost in my bedroom etc. Q3 – An estimate of the cost (a) in pounds and (b) in man hours it will have cost the force to investigate.

THE above request was submitted to Tayside Police by an anonymous investigator under the terms of the Freedom of Information Act, a piece of legislation that has brought to light many items of paranormal-related interest buried in official files. The police response states that 'a search of the Incident Recording System has been carried out for incidents including any of the words "UFO", "ghost", "witch", "vampire", or "zombie" to attempt to locate any incident reports which meet the criteria of the above request.' This search turned up a total of five reports, four of which related to alleged sightings of UFOs, none of which were spectacularly exciting. The fifth incident concerned a supposed assault by violent ghosts. In January 2009, an individual in Dundee claimed they were being attacked by ghosts within the house – following attendance by police officers, it was ascertained that the individual had been hallucinating.

So, not much joy for hunters after police-related paranormal events, then. The force also stated that they could not provide details of the costs and manpower hours that had been spent on the five incidents. The full response, which was posted online in May 2011, can be found on the force's website: www.tayside.police.uk.

Of course, the vast majority of individual encounters with the alleged supernatural are not reported to the police, who have far more important things to be dealing with anyway. In the Spring of 2011, I appealed, via the 'Craigie' column in the *Courier & Advertiser* and my own website and blog, for Dundonians to come forward with their personal spectral experiences. I am grateful to all those who responded, and for their permission to reproduce their fascinating and previously unpublished stories here (other personal stories from this appeal can be found in Chapter four).

The Gardener Returns

In 1987, June and Norrie Kelso moved into a new house in Belltree Gardens in Broughty Ferry. The estate had been built a year previously, on what had originally been strawberry fields. All was quiet at first, but then sometime in the early 1990s they started to notice a persistent odd sound at their kitchen door. June described it to me as: 'Someone coming in and wiping their feet.' At first they thought it was simply their son Derek arriving, but then it became clear that the noises continued when Derek was elsewhere in the house, or out altogether. To make things even stranger, the sounds kept to the timetable of someone working outdoors. Over the years it became apparent that they were never heard in the winter, only commencing around the end of March, and persisting through the spring and summer until the close of September, or the early weeks of October. During the colder and darker months the 'feet-wiping' took place at around 6 p.m., but during the summer months, the sounds did not manifest until about 9 p.m. And to top it all, they were heard every weekday, but only rarely on weekends. The Kelsos therefore came to the conclusion that the sounds originated from a gardener or farm labourer, returning to his bothy after the day's work, and they nicknamed their regular visitor 'Big Tam'.

One of the interesting aspects of this persistent audio phenomenon is that it was witnessed by more than the immediate family of June, Norrie and Derek. One night June's sister Ena, who lived in Edinburgh, was staying in the downstairs bedroom when she heard noises from the kitchen. She thought it was June making a cup of tea, but the kitchen was empty, and she became very scared when she realised that the noises had no obvious cause.

Irene, a family friend from the locality, also heard the noises, and was so upset that she burst out crying. Derek's former girlfriend, Claire, stayed overnight several times, and also reported the sounds. With six witnesses, it seems there was an objective reality to the phenomenon.

Out loud, June asked 'Big Tam' to leave the kitchen, and he did – only to simply move upstairs into the hall cupboard. Derek's bedroom was close by and he became scared by the noises that were now being heard at night, so June had more words with their spectral resident, who promptly decamped back to the kitchen. June then did some research on hauntings and read that spirits may not know that they are trapped between the realms of the living and the dead, and so need guidance to help them to depart. She told the spirit that it was stuck between two worlds, and was free to depart. Soon after, the noises ceased.

A while later, in 1997, in an apparently unrelated incident, June had a visionary experience of some kind of apparition or entity. Both Norrie and Derek were in the living room and June joined them to get glasses out of the cabinet. As she turned round, she saw an astonishing sight where the living room door and wall adjoined the dining room. This is how she described what she experienced:

> It was a woman with a very small oval face and shimmering with flowing silk from her head right down to the bottom, but with no face, if you know what I mean. There were no eyes etc. I'll never forget it as it was beautiful, like silk shimmering in the light, silvery grey and pale blue. I felt so calm and peaceful.

Her husband and son could both see that she was looking entranced at something that was invisible to the two of them. She was stock still, and only when the vision had faded away could she describe to them what she had seen. No further strange events occurred.

Intriguingly, the Kelsos noticed that they persistently felt fatigued and lethargic, as if something in the house was draining their energy. They even called in an expert to check if they had a gas leak that was slowly poisoning them. When the family moved house in February 1999, they felt newly energised, 'like a weight being lifted off our shoulders,' as June put it. This might suggest that something natural in the physical environment at the Belltree Gardens residence was somehow interacting with human physiology to create the haunting. On the other hand, perhaps the paranormal phenomenon – whatever it actually was, returning gardener or no – was indeed manifesting by drawing energy from the humans present.

A Mental Impression of a 'Butler'

This is a tantalising one-off episode that took place between September 1984 and August 1985, when Colin McLeod was employed as the supervisor of the Visitor Centre Project at Dundee University Botanic Garden. The project team occupied a studio in the semi-basement of 'Ardvreck', an expansive Edwardian pile at No. 516, Perth Road. The impressive house was built in 1907 for Harry Walker, a jute manufacturer at Caldrum Works; however, the house was altered in 1928. At the time of Colin's experience, the building was owned by the university, and the curator of the Botanic Garden lived in the flat directly above the workplace, with a stairwell linking the two levels.

The studio was light and sunny, with a view over the Botanic Garden. The studio and the stairs leading up to the curator's residence were at one end of the sub-basement, with the toilet down a corridor at the opposite end. One summer afternoon, Colin was working alone in the studio. He popped into the bathroom, and, in his own words, this is what he experienced when he returned:

> As I came out of the bathroom, I had an intense impression of a person: a tall, gaunt, grey-skinned elderly man, slightly stooped, wearing a very dark suit rather too big for him and very shiny black shoes. For some reason, I thought he seemed more like a butler, perhaps, rather than someone who would have owned such a large house, while he looked very ill, like someone dying of cancer (perhaps his clothes had fitted him once?). He came down the stairs, paused, glanced along the corridor (showing no sign that he noticed me standing in the doorway), then he went on into the studio. Which, of course, was empty when I got to it.

On the face of it, this might seem to be a description of an apparition, a figure that subscribes to the traditional idea of a 'ghost'. But Colin was adamant that what he experienced had no perceptual or objective reality, but was instead a mental impression of the figure – as if he had not seen it, but imagined it. Here is his description of this 'mental impression':

> I describe this incident as if I saw a physical person, or at least a 'physical' ghost, because it was so vivid and detailed, but it

was really a mental impression, as if imagined … For no reason I suddenly thought of this person very vividly, but I was fully aware that he wasn't actually a physical entity. For this reason, I didn't have any concern about going back into the studio a few seconds afterwards.

Why would Colin suddenly have had such a potent internal impression of this forlorn figure? He himself has no idea. The man was not someone out of his past; he was not thinking about him; he had never had a similar experience, nor has anything remotely akin occurred since. As for the location, none of the other members of staff had reported anything strange, and, as noted, the space was not in the slightest bit foreboding, being bright and airy.

Thinking about Ghosts

What does strike me about Colin's thoughtful analysis is that, in other hands, this could easily have been described as an encounter with a traditional ghost. Instead, the emphasis is on the internal experience, with a clear understanding that what he saw was the result of subjective 'mind-stuff' *in here*, rather than an objective, 'world-stuff' apparition *out there*. Which leads to the obvious question: how many ghosts are mistakenly reported as having a real-world existence – that is, we see them with our eyes because they appear to manifest *out there* – when in truth our visual perception plays no part in the experience, and what is 'seen' is actually an artefact created by the witness's own brain? How many 'ghosts' are actually generated by synaptic activity within our own neurological systems? What percentage of all the world's ghost sightings are born exclusively of our minds?

To most people, a ghost is a visual phenomenon, and the word 'ghost' means 'an apparition of a dead person'. Typically, ghosts are thought to be conscious, that is, they think and can respond to changes in their environment (such as when someone asks them a question). This latter notion also includes the assumption that not only are the ghostly-dead conscious, but that they can communicate with the living. Frequently, such communication takes place via a third party such as a medium, who becomes the channel through which the dead speak to us. All of this is based on what might be termed the 'Survival Hypothesis', that is, the idea that our consciousness survives death and continues to exist as a coherent thinking entity in some form of afterlife. The Survival Hypothesis is immensely popular, largely due to four overlapping factors: the lingering effects of religion; the grief of bereavement; sentimentality; and the towering hubris of our own egos – we cannot believe that something as unique as us can be extinguished for ever.

But clearly not all haunting phenomena fit these simplistic criteria. Sometimes no apparitions are seen, and only sounds or a sense of presence are noted. Other apparitions appear not to be conscious of their environment, and simply repeat a stereotyped set of actions again and again, as if they were a mere echo of a single episode – such repeating apparitions are called imprints, as the idea is that they are somehow imprinted on the physical environment. Not all reports of ghosts support the Survival Hypothesis.

In general, if someone reports seeing an apparition, the immediate reaction is to make the link: apparition = ghost = conscious spirit of a dead person. This is certainly the way sightings of apparitions and similar experiences are usually treated in the press. And the various opinions of mediums and psychics are also given the standard analysis that voices/words from beyond means communication from the conscious spirit of a dead person. But research into paranormal phenomena has progressed in recent years, attracting the attention of parapsychologists, physicists, psychiatrists, and other professionals from the medical and scientific fields. The Survival Hypothesis is no longer the only way to think about ghosts. Even if only a small percentage of the vast anecdotal material concerning ghosts is authentic, then clearly something is going on. But what that 'something' is may be more complex than the standard notion that the dead are returning to haunt us.

I suspect that there is a continuity of internal 'ghostly' experiences in the three incidents described so far in this chapter. At the negative end of the spectrum is the person who called the police for protection against malevolent ghosts – ghosts that only existed within the pulse of electrical signals within that witness's brain. At the opposite end of the spectrum comes June Kelso's vision of a beautiful but faceless being, a radiant experience with a beatific and entirely positive emotional result. And in the middle we have Colin McLeod's mental impression of a fully-formed apparition, an experience that had minimal emotional or cognitive impact precisely because his self-awareness informed him that the figure was a construct.

None of this means that ghosts are 'all in the mind', or that all reports of apparitions imply some kind of mental illness. On the contrary, it is yet another lesson that teaches us to be aware of simplistic and credulous views about the supernatural. Much of the external universe remains to be explained,

and part of that mystery certainly includes the question of ghosts and the afterlife. But on the other hand, a significant quantity of alleged 'paranormal events' are clearly generated by our own neurology – an internal landscape that we are only tentatively starting to explore and understand. Neuroscience is now the cutting edge of paranormal research.

Physiology, Psychiatry and the Paranormal

For example, let's look at the pioneering work of James McHarg. Dr McHarg was a consultant and honorary senior lecturer in the Department of Psychiatry of Dundee University, and a consultant psychiatrist at the Royal Dundee Liff Hospital. As part of a long and distinguished career, he was also a Fellow of the Royal College of Physicians of Edinburgh and a Foundation Fellow of the Royal College of Psychiatrists. He died in 2003, aged eighty-six.

In his later working years, Dr McHarg became intrigued by some of his psychiatric patients who reported paranormal-type experiences. Unwilling to dismiss such reports as just part of the patients' illness-related unreality, he analysed the cases with typical intellectual rigour, and later wrote several papers for the Society for Psychical Research (he also lectured to the Senior Fellows of the Royal College of Physicians of Edinburgh on the subject of poltergeists, which must have been an interesting evening).

Although the names and personal details of his patients were of course protected by medical confidentiality, most of the people concerned came from the Dundee area, and hence their cases are of particular interest here. Some of Dr McHarg's most penetrating insights came in a 1982 article for the Journal of the Society of Psychical Research, entitled, 'The Paranormal and the Recognition of Personal Distress'. Here he discussed the connection between 'personal distress' – either mental illness or physiological symptoms (damage to the mind or the body) – and experiences which were paranormal in nature, or at least had the appearance of being so. He distinguished between two sets of phenomena:

1) Pseudo psi-phenomena, caused by objective disturbance. Here the medical condition of the patient generated phenomena which on the surface appeared to be paranormal, but which were, in fact, entirely subjective and 'non-real'.

2) Genuine psi-phenomena arising out of subjective distress or objective disturbance. Here, in a small number of cases, the medical condition of the patient seemed to be linked to phenomena that appeared to be entirely authentic.

Pseudo Psi-Phenomena in Medical Cases

As examples of pseudo psi-phenomena, McHarg looked at both physiological and psychiatric issues. Within the latter, he included the delusions and hallucinations reported by people with severe mental illness (such as schizophrenia and paranoid psychoses), as well as cases where patients have 'fits', or enter trances or other altered states. Other, less serious conditions, known as 'sub-delirious states', can leave the patient acting normally at most times but subject to hallucinations, especially in the evening or at night. Typically, such hallucinations will feature moving objects or figures seen in the corner of the eye, in the peripheral field of vision. Other visual and tactile hallucinations – such as the sense of being touched by invisible or ghostly hands – can be brought on by drug use or alcohol withdrawal. Further down the severity scale, bereavement can have a powerful short-term mental impact on some people, and part of the psychiatric expression of this impact may include hallucinations of the recently deceased.

On the physiological front, McHarg investigated the impact of ischaemia, a condition in which the blood vessels in the brainstem start to harden, leading to a reduction in the blood supply to the brain. A number of ischaemia patients – all elderly ladies living alone – reported seeing apparitions in their own home. The 'ghost people' lounged around the house, doing and saying nothing, just sitting in chairs, while the patient largely ignored them, sometimes cleaning and tidying up around them while the figures remained seated and stationary. Not surprisingly, the patients were distressed to find silent strangers occupying their homes, and the reactions – especially the notion that the uninvited guests were harbingers of death – can be easily imagined. Sadly such experiences, diagnostic of ischaemic illness when the patient was otherwise mentally healthy, were usually hints that a further decline was on the cards.

Also of ghost-related interest was the impact of the brain disturbance known as temporal lobe epilepsy, or TLE. The temporal lobes are the part of the brain that deals with areas such as our emotions, our sense of 'who we are', and our perception of sound, smell and sight, and many aspects of memory. Clearly, disruption to this part of the brain has the potential to 'mess' with some key aspects of our mental experience, including what we think we see, smell, feel and remember. In some ways, the term 'temporal lobe epilepsy' is unfortunate, as although it refers to a temporary electrical disturbance, there are no grand mal fits that many people associate with the word 'epilepsy', and in many cases the symptoms may be so subtle that only a trained professional such as a psychiatrist will be able to spot them.

One of McHarg's patients had experiences that in other circumstances would have been reported as an encounter with a ghost. Frank, a young man in his twenties, had persistent visitations from his father, who had died when he was five years old. The figure appeared in broad daylight dressed in his naval uniform, and father and son had multiple two-way conversations, in which the young man learned many things about his father's life and experiences. Frank's mother confirmed that he could not have known about these events, as he had been so young when his father died. On the face of it, then, the patient was in regular communication with his dead father. McHarg, however, identified the cause of the hallucinations as a head injury from a few years before. The damage had resulted in what was called post-traumatic temporal lobe epilepsy, and with the appropriate medication the hallucinations ceased.

As the apparition of the father was 'non-real', McHarg wondered whether some of the 'unknowable' facts Frank had related had derived from early-life telepathic contact between father and son, prior to his demise. He concluded, however, that the majority of the communications had their source in the young boy's real-world experience – for example, from overhearing adult conversations – and had been cloaked by cryptomnesia, the process involving the occlusion of long-term memory. The temporary lobe epilepsy had stimulated the 'forgotten' memories into vivid reminiscence, and they only appeared paranormal because of their association with the visitations by the father's apparition. In a letter to the *Journal of the Society of Psychical Research* in June 1979, McHarg noted that three of his young temporal lobe epilepsy out-patients were currently reporting apparitions of the dead, and that all three were clearly hallucinating. He reported that:

> Everyone has a store of past perceptual experiences, or fantasies, of persons close to them who, with the passing years, increasingly are deceased persons. Such stored experiences are always ready, with hypoxic stimulation of the specially vulnerable regions of the temporal lobes, to pop into consciousness with striking vividness.

In another of McHarg's TLE-related cases, a patient, who was otherwise mentally normal, was convinced he was being tormented by a poltergeist. So bad was the problem that he had asked a priest to conduct an exorcism. The episodes had commenced in August 1978, when the tormenting spirit poked what felt like a finger in the man's left ear and said to him, 'I am a poltergeist and I have come back to haunt you!' This was followed by screams, screeches and what he called a 'racketty noise'. Then there was a flash of light to the left, which resembled the face of the man's deceased father. On later occasions he experienced the same voice, plus more screeching, and persistent scratching at the wall.

Once again it is obvious that some people – including I dare say a proportion of paranormal investigators – would have concluded that the man was suffering a genuine visitation of a ghostly nature. However, the man's GP referred him to McHarg, whose sessions elucidated two key facts: firstly, the patient reported perceiving numerous anomalous smells, such as acid, urine or faeces; and secondly, his medical history showed he had suffered severe injury to the right side of his head. The right temporal lobe is associated with perceptions – such as smell, vision and hearing – in the nostril, eye and ear on the left side of the head; and all of the patient's symptoms were concentrated on the left side. McHarg concluded that the head injury was the ultimate cause of the hallucinations, and nothing paranormal was involved.

Yet another TLE 'ghostly' hallucination analysed by McHarg in his professional capacity was presented at the annual convention of the Parapsychological Association in Utrecht in 1976, and appeared in Andrew Mackenzie's authoritative 1987 book on paranormal experiences, *The Seen and the Unseen.*

On the Saturday afternoon of 28 June 1969, Mrs Jean Bennett – not her real name – was being shown round her friend's new home. As she made her way around, she suddenly caught a whiff of a 'milky' smell and entered what she called a 'switched off' state. She then saw a female figure standing in the far corner of the dining room. The woman was standing as if stirring a pot on a cooker, although no stove was visible. She had brown hair and a bronzed complexion, and was wearing a long black dress covered with a black pinafore at the waist. Her head was turned over her shoulder and she was looking directly at Jean with an astonished expression.

Although the day was warm and sunny, Jean felt as cold as ice, and the skin on the back of her neck tingled. Her friend, who had seen nothing, suggested carrying on with the tour, but Jean, whose eyes were now welling with tears, blurted out, 'I can't go yet.' Only when the apparition vanished did she describe her experience. The householder turned pale at the mention of the cooker – they had recently renovated

and the stove had stood at exactly that spot. Further research found that the house had previously been occupied by two sisters by the name of Blair (pseudonym), who had been teachers – and a Miss Blair had been at Jean's mother's primary school. When Jean and her friend contacted a former teacher at the school, Jean, unprompted, picked Miss Blair out of an old photograph – and identified her as the woman she had seen stirring an invisible pot.

On the face of it, Jean had seen the ghost of a former occupant of her friend's house. But later, when she became one of McHarg's out-patients, the psychiatrist dug further. During the Second World War, Jean had experienced brief olfactory and thermal hallucinations – such as the smell of carnations, or a sensation of warmth and pleasure. The doctor suspected that she suffered from mild TLE, and linked this to the smell of milk just before the vision of the woman. Then he discovered that Jean's mother had died in 1955 – was it possible that, at that time, Jean had visited the house to tell her mother's former teacher of the death? And had this memory lain dormant for years, only to be prompted into vivid reminiscence by the brief attack of TLE? The linkage of events was uncertain and speculative, especially when it was later discovered that the cooker in the dining room had only been installed in that location after the Misses Blair had left the house. But McHarg considered he was on stronger ground with a diagnosis of mild TLE, as indicated by the milky smell and the 'switched off' feeling.

So, Frank had not been visited by his dead father; Jean had not seen the spirit of a deceased teacher; elderly ladies had not been invaded by uninvited guests; the bereaved patients had not seen the ghosts of their loved ones; and a man looking for an exorcist had not been tormented by a malevolent poltergeist. But all these cases were only given a medical diagnosis due to the diligence and professionalism of Dr McHarg. And we only know about them because his interest in paranormal topics drove him to give presentations and write papers on the cases, so that others would benefit from his experience.

If circumstances had been different, however, any one of these cases could have become, entirely falsely, a 'ghost story', which conceivably could have made the patients' condition worse, or at least delayed a proper diagnosis. It thus behoves responsible paranormal investigators to take great care when assessing individual cases, because mental disorder or neurological problems could be a factor. This is made more difficult because, as noted, although florid disorders will be obvious to most observers, some more subtle conditions can only be diagnosed through careful medical or psychiatric analysis. Matters are made worse because of the stigma attached to mental illness and even temporary disorders of the brain. No witness to a paranormal event will welcome the suggestion that they are hallucinating, as this phrase is still regarded as cognate with 'being mad'. Experiencing transient hallucinations does not make you 'mad'; it merely means that part of your cognitive or neurological system is temporarily not functioning properly. Few in the general public have an appreciation of either the complexity of the human mind, or what can easily go wrong with various parts of our brain, perception processes, or memories. If anyone involved in a paranormal case thinks that a witness is suffering some kind of objective disturbance, then the best practice would be to withdraw from the case and suggest that the person concerned consult their general practitioner.

Genuine Psi-Phenomena in Medical Cases

As for Dr McHarg's second category, 'Genuine psi-phenomena arising out of subjective distress or objective disturbance', he found fewer cases. But, given that they were thoroughly investigated and witnessed, they might have much to tell us. Before looking at these cases, though, it is worth starting with a statement that McHarg made in the 1982 article in the *Journal of the Society of Psychical Research*:

> Genuine paranormal phenomena are no more common in the mentally disturbed than in the population generally. Certainly the mentally disturbed, while they not infrequently report pseudopsi … do not commonly report genuine psi. On the other hand, some experiences of seriously disturbed patients, which they themselves do not interpret as paranormal, have seemed to psychiatrists investigating them to have a genuinely paranormal basis.

The phrase 'Genuine psi-phenomena arising out of subjective distress' could be a virtual definition of many poltergeist cases, where the phenomena often appear to focus on a disturbed individual, such as an adolescent going through puberty, or a member of the household who is under great strain. McHarg described one Dundee poltergeist case, without giving any names or dates. The phenomena had included the extensive movement of objects, including the toppling of a heavy bookcase. The family history showed that child sexual abuse had taken place. Once the family were attending a clinic, a medical and social solution was reached, and the phenomena ceased. Sadly, from our point of view, the doctor concerned in the case considered that the paranormal events were not her concern, and so did not investigate them further. McHarg, who was of the opinion that a small number of paranormal reports were genuine, thought that this attitude, although understandable, could lead to a mistaken diagnosis in a few cases – for example, a person suffering genuine supernatural assaults could be misdiagnosed as schizophrenic.

The second example of what McHarg regarded as genuine phenomena was described in his paper 'Cryptomnesic and Paranormal Personation'. Forty-four-year-old Mrs Margaret D. had a long history of admissions for what was then called manic depression. On 4 August 1967, she was at a Dundee psychiatric hospital for a relatively mild to moderate depressive episode, and had spent a comfortable, mostly undisturbed day. At around 6.15 p.m., in a calm state, she went for a walk in the grounds with her husband. But at around 7.25 p.m. her condition seemed to change, and about ten minutes later she became very disturbed, shouting and swearing and insisting that she had to get to her father's house. It was with difficulty that her husband, assisted by the nurses, managed to persuade her to return to the ward.

The following day, a Saturday, Mrs D., as was usual, returned home; her husband looked after her at weekends. The couple went to visit her parents, but there was no reply. It later emerged that Mrs D.'s father had died of a stroke the night before. The time of death was uncertain, but it was probably around 7.35 p.m., just when the disturbance took place at the hospital some miles away.

On 16 August, twelve days after the events, McHarg interviewed Mrs D. and asked her for her account of the episode. She told him that she had first experienced a severe headache and then a floating feeling, and shortly after felt a strong compulsion to visit her father. The next moment she felt as if she was actually in her father's house. Her father himself was not visible, and the room was empty. When asked if she had the feeling that her father had died, the response was emphatically 'no'. Instead, she told McHarg that she had the overwhelming sensation that she herself had died.

Mrs D. and her father were very close. McHarg posited that, at the moment of death, the old man had somehow communicated with his daughter in such a way that she 'personated' him. In other words, for the few minutes while her body was in great distress in the hospital grounds, and her mind was in distress looking round the apparently empty house, the respective consciousnesses of father and daughter were effectively linked. In McHarg's opinion, at the time, Mrs D. felt she was in her father's house, and felt that she herself had just died – she could not see her father because, in a sense, she was him.

three

Malevolent Entities

THE following stories all have one thing in common – the entities that were encountered were far from friendly...

Dundee Backpackers

Hurrying shoppers and commuters usually ignore the five-storey building at No. 71 High Street, but hidden behind its plain façade is an architectural history lesson almost unique in Dundee. The structure is actually a complex of three different but linked buildings, looming like miniature skyscrapers around a miniscule inner courtyard. Known as Gardyne's Land after the building's first recorded owner, John Gardyne, the earliest part dates to the 1560s; however, there were significant additions in the 1640s and onwards into the Victorian period. Having lain empty since 1980, it has now been fully restored and operates as the Dundee Backpackers Hostel. Many original features have been retained and there is a small exhibition open to the public. It is a powerfully atmospheric place.

The age and atmosphere of the labyrinthine hostel occasionally seems to rub off on the guests. Sometime in 2010, a woman checked in and promptly checked out again, saying there was no way she could stay in the room, which gave her 'the creeps'. She lost her advance deposit

Gardyne's Land, High Street, now the Dundee Backpackers Hostel. (The Author)

The rear of Gardyne's Land in the 1890s, from Lamb's Dundee: Its Quaint and Historic Buildings *(Perth & Kinross Libraries)*

and immediately set off to find alternative accommodation. Every now and then the staff hear rumours from the guests that the hostel is haunted, but nothing substantive has been forthcoming. However, there is one exception.

Grant Anderson, from Glasgow, stayed at the hostel over Christmas 2010, and a couple of weeks later submitted his experience to the website www.ghost-story.co.uk/yourstories. Grant had been visiting his brother and knew the hostel well. Although he was virtually the only guest – he only saw two people over three days – he was not concerned, as he had never felt uncomfortable at the hostel; but all that was to change. After spending Christmas Day with his brother, he found it impossible to get to sleep in the hostel that night, experiencing a continual sense of being watched, and later on becoming overwhelmed with a sense of despair and loneliness. He then slept right through Boxing Day, beset by ghastly nightmares, before getting up around 3 a.m. on the 27th. Hunger drove him out at 5.45 a.m. but, after failing to find anywhere open, he returned to his room, which had a window view through to the games room.

The games room was usually a blaze of light, and he had been in it just a few hours earlier, but now it was pitch black. Puzzled, he scanned the deep darkness and spotted a 'soft fuzzy glow of light'. As he studied this one light source, it resolved itself into a grimacing human-like face with hideous eyes. In his opinion it was: 'Pure evil. Some sort of demonic humanoid entity.'

Grant did not react with fear. Instead, he went to the kitchen and calmly made himself a cup of tea. Only on returning to his room did a feeling of horror start to overcome him. Still he did not panic, but in a controlled manner folded up the duvet and rental towel, all the while desperate to get out quickly. As he departed, he noticed that the games room was its usual lit-up self. Upon returning to Glasgow, he found his imagination invaded by the evil face. He was scared by the slightest sounds and was considering visiting a priest.

The Ghost Through the Wall

In the autumn of 1974, an Orkney lass named Shirley Brown arrived in Dundee to study nursing. After six months, she took up residence in a tenement flat on Morgan Street, her flatmate being a fellow student-nurse called Gail Bruce. For a time nothing was remiss with the tiny flat, which consisted of just a living room/kitchen, a bathroom and the shared bedroom. Then, one night in January 1976, Gail was unable to sleep. About 3.30 a.m. or so, the hall light came on, and she heard the distinct sound of someone slowly padding about the bathroom. Frightened that someone had broken in, she hid beneath the bedclothes. After a few minutes she realised that the front door was solidly locked and the hall was now in darkness, so she peeped out. Standing beside Shirley's bed was an elderly woman with short grey hair and wearing a nightgown or long dress, pale blue in colour. She appeared to be whispering to Shirley, but although Gail could not make out the words, she felt a terrible sensation of evil and menace. The nurse closed her eyes briefly, and, when she re-opened them, the figure was gone. Gail was too frightened to sleep, and in the morning got up much earlier than usual for work, leaving Shirley asleep, as her flatmate's shift did not start until 1 p.m. At lunchtime, Gail returned to the flat and told Shirley what she had seen. Concerned, they both decided not to be in the flat alone.

A week passed with no further incident. Then one night, a little before midnight, Shirley was reading in bed when she heard padding footsteps in the kitchen – just as Gail had heard previously. Shirley was frightened because she knew Gail was in the bathroom, but, hoping against hope that her friend had slipped into the kitchen, she tapped on the wall, willing Gail to tap back. Instead, the response was a terrifying barrage of noise, as if something with superhuman strength was attempting to break through the wall. Hearing Shirley's call, Gail rushed in from the bathroom, at which point the noises abruptly ceased. The pair sat in petrified silence for a time, and then the aural assault continued, this time lasting for more than a quarter of an hour.

At this point, the two girls had had enough. Even though it was nearing 1 a.m., they resolved to quit the flat straightaway. Hastily throwing together clothes, they were about to leave when, with sinking hearts, they remembered that the keys for the front door were in the kitchen – the source of the noises. As they raced into the hall, adrenaline coursing through their veins, the light bulb blew with a bright-blue flash, so in the darkness they grabbed the keys from the kitchen table and fled out of the door.

That night the pair stayed with friends, returning in daylight to pack their clothes before leaving for good. An inspection showed that the kitchen wall, apparently the subject of an all-out attack the night before, was entirely unmarked.

The story was first gathered by author Peter Moss for his 1977 book, *Ghosts Over Britain*. Further details emerged in *Is Anybody There?*, an investigation into the paranormal by Stewart Lamont, published in 1980 (both works are highly recommended for anyone wanting to learn more about hauntings in Scotland and elsewhere in Britain). Mr Lamont visited the flat, and found that no further disturbances had been recorded. The family living there suggested that the ghost, or whatever it was, may have been connected with the old Dundee Royal Lunatic Asylum. The asylum was established on a site between what are now Albert Street, Cardean Street and Morgan Street; opening its doors in 1820, it was demolished roughly sixty years later, when the facility relocated to Liff. If you are looking for an 'origin event' for a frenzied supernatural attack, I suppose you could do worse than focus on a place for the severely disturbed. But I have an alternative candidate.

On 30 January 1935, the *Scotsman* reported that three elderly sisters had been found dead at a house on Morgan Street. Misses Emily, Martha and Jesse Miller had succumbed to gas poisoning. The kitchen was full of gas, both a gaslight mantle and the taps of the gas cooker being turned on. Matches were scattered over the floor next to the cooker. One of the ladies was lying in bed, with her sister seated on a chair behind her. The third sister had collapsed in front of the stove. They had been dead for two days. Emily Miller, who at fifty-nine years old was the youngest of the three, had been a teacher for thirty-eight years, last working at Logie Central School.

It was intended to perform a post-mortem on Martha, the lady in the bed, as she had been ill for some time, and it was possible she had expired of natural causes rather than being suffocated by the fumes. In the end, it was decided that no such examination was necessary, and, on 1 February, the tragic trio were buried in the same grave at the Eastern Cemetery. A crowd of 3,000 people lined the funeral route. The *Scotsman* carried follow-ups on the story on 31 January and 2 February.

If you wish to construct a scenario in which an elderly lady launches a last desperate attempt to escape as her room fills with gas, and then transfer that as an origin narrative to the events of January 1976, be my guest.

The Craigie Poltergeist

'A TERRIFIED FAMILY CLAIMED LAST NIGHT THEY HAVE BEEN FORCED OUT OF THEIR HOME – BY A POLTERGEIST.'

That was the headline in the *Sun* on 14 November 2008. According to the report, Tony Ritchie and Rose Cameron had fled their council house in Mid Craigie because of violent attacks by a poltergeist. The couple shared the house with their daughter, Leanne, and her partner, Colin, who had an infant son, Cody. The phenomena started when Cody was born and was brought home, ten weeks previously.

A fortnight after the baby arrived, Tony started suffering supernatural assaults. He was thrown 3ft against the kitchen units, was pushed down the stairs, and in the kitchen felt as if he had been punched in the face. Things seemed to calm down after the house was blessed by a Revd Vincent Coyne, but, after ten days' respite, the phenomena returned, albeit relatively innocuously – two ceramic pigs were found relocated on the stairs, even though no one had moved them. The ornaments seemed to be a favourite item for the poltergeist, as later events proved.

At this point, the malevolence of the phenomena escalated. The words 'You must go' were found scrawled on a wall, and the message 'Gonna hurt you' appeared on a notepad. Baby Cody's cradle started to rock for no reason; the infant's clothes were found scattered over the floor; slash marks appeared in Colin's bed, posters, T-shirts and towel, as well as in a bedroom carpet; and, most frightening of all, Cody was moved by unknown forces. Colin and Leanne had left the ten-week-old infant on their double bed while they were in the bathroom. When they went back to check on Cody, he was off the bed and lying beside the bathroom door – with an ornamental ceramic pig on his chest.

This was the last straw for the young couple, and Colin and Leanne decamped to Edinburgh. After they left, Tony and Rose came across more disturbing evidence in Cody's cradle – a Rangers doll lying next to an 8in carving knife. There was a Bible at the foot of the cradle. Some time afterwards, Tony and Rose also fled the house, and claimed they were facing homelessness because Angus Housing refused to allocate them a new council house.

Sadly, the story was not followed up by the *Sun* or indeed any other newspaper, and I have been unable to trace the participants, so we only have a very limited view on the episode. As a result, any analysis can be merely speculative. Many poltergeist cases appear to centre round a troubled teenager in the house, a person known as the 'focus'. This, of course, does not explain how the poltergeist mechanism operates, or why certain phenomena erupt – the connection between teenagers and poltergeist phenomena is merely one of observation, not explanation. Leanne, Cody's mother, was eighteen – could she have been the 'focus'? (This of course is not certain, as there are known cases where the poltergeist has no obvious adolescent focus.) Other factors could have been at play, such as possible religious tensions – note that a Catholic priest was called in, while Colin, as is clear from the report, was a Rangers supporter. In addition, there are always questions that arise when disputes over council homes and re-housing are publicised. And finally, I note that the South Shields poltergeist, subject of a superb book by Michael Hallowell and Darren Ritson, received a great deal of publicity in the summer of 2008. With all these factors in play, it is difficult to go beyond the bare reports of the disturbing incidents and come to any kind of conclusion.

Another council house ghost appeared in the *Sun* on 5 September 2001, although here the effects on the occupant were far less serious. 'Anne-Marie' from Dundee wrote to the paper's psychic, Katie Coutts, about the 'depressed' ghost that was overwhelming her with waves of sadness. The previous tenant had had a dreadful period in her final years – her husband died, her son was murdered and the killer never caught, and then she died of cancer, alone. Anne-Marie was convinced that the spirit of the woman was still in the house: 'Lately, when I've been in the house alone, I feel this great sadness. Often it can be overwhelming and I have been very depressed.' She had asked the council for a transfer, but had been refused because her situation was not a priority. The paper's psychic suggested having the house blessed, or speaking aloud, telling the spirit she was sorry about the suffering she had gone through.

The A92 Apparition

About 1982, a woman and her son took a holiday in Scotland, travelling up from their home in the Malvern Hills, with each driving in turns. By the time they reached Dundee, and were driving on the A92 towards Arbroath, it was well into the night. The son, sitting in the passenger seat,

spotted a woman by the side of the road, and suggested they stop and give her a lift. But then he shouted, 'It's a ghost; put your foot on the accelerator!' As they passed the figure, the driver took a good look at the pedestrian, and gave a truly bizarre description: 'Although it was pitch dark, her head was lit up like a balloon. It was as if she had a light inside. She had this beautiful smile on her face but her face was fluorescent!' Both the driver and her son were deeply frightened by the experience.

This odd and anonymous episode appeared in a 2002 book by Anne Bradford and David Taylor, *Haunted Holidays*. There are no more details; so, once again, it is difficult to comment. The lit-up woman could have been someone playing a prank, or the travellers, fatigued by their long journey, could have misidentified something else by the roadside. The fact that both of them saw something strange suggests that there was indeed a figure by the roadside – but was it really a fluorescent phantom?

The Shopping Spook

The Wellgate Shopping Centre can hardly be described as one of Dundee's loveliest buildings. The construction of the mall flattened a number of old tenements and shops at the bottom of the Hilltown, and irrevocably spoiled the setting of the adjacent eighteenth-century St Andrew's Church. Ever since the soulless behemoth opened in April 1978, there have been rumours that it is haunted. 'GHOSTLY NOISES IN WELLGATE TERRIFY CLEANERS' was the headline in the *Courier & Advertiser* on 25 August 1978. Earlier in the week a fire alarm went off and staff on the 9 p.m. to 7.30 a.m. cleaning shift heard footsteps on the roof. The police were called but found

nothing. Then staff heard voices coming from a lift shaft in an unoccupied part of the locked and closed centre. Once again police did not encounter any intruders, although one officer said he had heard the voices. The cleaners told the reporter that they were so frightened that one had taken to carrying a large stick. Another cleaner said: 'We have heard voices and footsteps, and fire doors have been mysteriously found open for no apparent reason.' Alexander Johnston said he had detected a 'supernatural presence' in the Wellgate during his regular local spiritualist meeting, and so came straightaway to the shopping centre, arriving at the same time as the police. 'I think I know who is responsible for these happenings,' he said. 'They are two people who were associated with this area and the project, both of whom have died recently.' It should be noted that spiritualists, as adherents of a religion based around communication with the dead, will always favour the Survival Hypothesis as an explanation for hauntings. In contrast, veteran ghost-hunter Andrew Green, writing in his book *Ghosts of Today*, speculated that the cause of the disturbances was a poltergeist force associated with a living person working in the mall.

On 2 November 2007, the *Courier & Advertiser* interviewed centre manager John Morton: 'I've been here since 1990 and a lot of people have told me they think the centre might be haunted,' he said. He continued:

I've heard that the ghost walks the north end of the building on the third floor [by the Wellgate Steps exit]… everybody who thinks they might have seen or felt something says it happens around 3 a.m. when they are alone. It begins with a feeling that someone is watching them but when they turn around there is nobody there. This continues to happen and the presence becomes stronger. The temperature drops dramatically too.

Given that the phenomenon has a consistent timeframe and physical component, I suggest it is a consequence of the centre's early-morning environment. Perhaps something switches on that accidentally generates ultrasound – sound below the level of human hearing that can make people feel as if someone is watching or even touching them. Or possibly there is some acoustic or electromagnetic effect in the echoing spaces that sets off the spooky feeling. The phenomenon definitely has the air of something with an environmental cause.

On the other hand – and when dealing with the paranormal there is always an 'on the other hand', few phenomena being simply explained – one late-night cleaner interviewed for the 2007 article added smells and apparitions to the mix:

> After you feel the presence there is a smell of violets and this permeates for a while and the feeling of being watched becomes more intense. Not many people have seen the ghost, but once someone saw an elderly lady wearing Victorian style clothes, and they were frozen to the spot.

And another cleaner was quoted as saying: 'I was walking and I felt as if someone was behind me. Then after a while it felt like it had walked right through me – it wasn't a very nice feeling.' I still suspect that the source is environmental, but you never know.

four

The Den o'Mains

ON an evening in the early summer of 1959 or 1960, nineteen-year-old Sarah Fraser was sitting on a bench in the Den o'Mains with her boyfriend Robert (now her husband). Robert was describing the sounds around them – the wind sighing though the trees and the gurgle of running water in the burn – when he asked her if she could hear the sound of wheels on gravel. She couldn't, and had a passing thought that he was trying to scare her. A little later, both Sarah and Robert heard wheels crunching on gravel quite loudly. From where they were sitting, on a slight incline beside a path, they had a view down each direction. Looking up to see the expected cyclist, they instead saw a tall man accompanying a woman pushing a pram, passing so close to the bench that Sarah could have reached out and touched them. Her boyfriend asked them what time it was, but the couple ignored him. Sarah and Robert glanced away for a moment to discuss how rude the couple were – but when they looked back, the pair, plus the pram, were nowhere to be seen, even though there was nowhere they could have hidden, and no time for them to have physically moved out of sight. The sound of the wheels had also ceased.

When she contacted me in June 2011, this is how Sarah described what she had seen:

> The man had a stovepipe hat and a jacket like a morning jacket with tails – the tails were very long, almost to his feet. The woman had a very long fitted coat with a small bustle at the back and you could see only a few inches of her skirt which was down to her shoes. Her hat was wide brimmed but pulled down at the sides by a veil which was tied under her chin. They were both very tall and slim and dressed completely in black. She was holding the pram with its handle at her chest level, the pram was very narrow but very deep with small wheels. The handle was part of the curve of the pram.

Sarah and Robert had been sitting on a south-facing bench on the north side of the Den, above one of the ponds that forms a small cascade. The time was around 8/9 p.m., the evening was still light, and visual conditions were clear. The spectral couple and pram approached from the west and were heading in the direction of the graveyard to the east. Despite the antique appearance of both the pram and

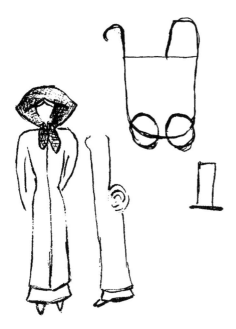

Sarah Fraser's 2011 drawing of the apparitions seen in Den o' Mains in 1959. Two views of the woman, one showing the bustle at the back; the short and deep pram; and the man's stovepipe hat. (Sarah Fraser)

the clothes worn by the man and woman, neither Sarah nor Robert thought there was anything strange about the pair as they were approaching. It was only when the pair disappeared that the young witnesses, in discussion together, realised that the couple did not fit with the modern world. This phenomenon, where people perceive extraordinary events as if they were merely commonplace and only later 'notice' the bizarre nature of what they have witnessed, is a factor common in many paranormal encounters. It is as if part of our brain has a filter which says, 'that can't be abnormal, therefore it is normal', and only after the incident has passed do we remove the filter and 'wake up' to what really happened. Despite the incident lasting just a brief time, it made a huge impact on Sarah and Robert, and they have a clear recollection of the details all these decades later. Neither had ever heard of anything spooky associ-

ated with the Den, and this has been the sole supernatural event in their lives.

This singular, one-off encounter with a pair of apparitions, complete with sound effects, is just one of a series of paranormal experiences that have been recorded in the Den o'Mains, a small gully that runs through Caird Park, the public green space donated to the city by Sir James Caird in the 1920s. North of the Kingsway, the park has an athletic stadium, a velodrome, a golf course and playing fields, and is bisected by a minor road serving all these facilities. Sporty and popular, it initially seems an unlikely locus for hauntings. But in the middle of the park is the Den o'Mains, a small ravine channelling the Gully Burn (often known as the Dichty Burn). Here, the open spaces of the park close in, hemmed about by trees and other vegetation. The Den has a different feel to the rest of the park. Towering above the south bank of this miniature glen is the striking edifice of Mains Castle, while opposite, on the north side, is the old graveyard of the now-vanished Mains Church.

The Graveyard of Mains

This slightly desolate walled cemetery sits hard against the northern lip of the burn, its tombstone ground sloping sharply into the ravine. The parish was amalgamated with that of Strathmartine in 1799, and, after a new church was built at Trottick a mile to the west two years later, the church at Mains was left to decay. At one point, a part of the ruin was converted into the burial vault of the Graham family. This mausoleum incorporated two old stone coffins secured at the corners with iron cramps, the clumsy boxes traditionally (but probably erroneously) said to have been built for victims of the plague. Nowadays, the coffins have gone and even the foundations of the kirk barely remain, although a medieval grave slab was rescued and is in the McManus Galleries. Nearby there was once a hamlet – Kirktown – with a manse, school, schoolhouse, and a handful of cottages, but all this has long vanished, the manse building the last to go, lasting until the 1940s. Time has also swept away the castle's dovecots and a stand of huge trees, including beech and oaks. Go on a misty day and the abandoned graveyard, with its toppled tombstones and slabs carved with skulls, is the epitome of a melancholic song by a gloomy Goth band.

All of this would seem to be a suitable mulch in which stories of ghosts can grow, and yet I can only find the vaguest of hints of such – certainly no recorded sightings or other experiences. There is a rumour that the burn – or the graveyard – is supposedly haunted by the spirit of a woman who committed suicide after escaping from Maryfield Hospital, which stood on the west side of Mains Loan until the early 1970s. It was opened in the 1890s to care for the indigent, the sick, and 'lunatics', but the building had been a poorhouse since the 1850s. Maryfield provided many services during its lifetime, from general admissions to maternity and mental health. It is conceivable that a disturbed person did escape and kill themselves, and that this shocking episode, barely remembered through the haze of time, gave rise to the notion that her spirit remains behind. However, I have been unable to find any example of what we might term the 'origin death' for this reputed ghost, and the alleged spectre itself eludes documented accounts so far.

The only ghost from the graveyard is a literary one. Dundee poet Joseph Lee (1876-1949) gives us a traditional moral tale in his 1910 volume *Tales o' Our Town*, with 'Pedlar Auld Jock Law. His Ghostly Encounter at Midnight with Bailie Braw in the Auld Kirkyaird o' Mains'. On a dark and stormy night, pedlar Jock Law seeks shelter

The old graveyard of Mains, with Mains Castle visible across the Den o' Mains. (The Author)

Mains Castle in 1910. (The Author)

The six-storey tower that dominates Mains Castle. (Author's collection)

beneath a gravestone, only to be dragged into a grave by the man commemorated on the slab, Bailie Braw:

> Come into the grave an' speak wi' me,
> For I've but a lanely weird to dree.

Dead for almost two centuries, Bailie Braw, formerly a great man in Dundee, needs to confess his sins. He abused women, he cheated, he stole and he robbed the poor, and, just as he reached the peak of his greedy ambition, he died. And he has been meditating on the human condition ever since:

> Some be wha say the dead do dwell
> Harpin' in heaven or howlin' in hell
> Heed nae, Gehenna's in oorsel',
> An' tho' the banes an' body rot,
> There is the worm which dieth not.

Standing in the lonely graveyard, you have a fine view of its neighbour across the ravine – Mains Castle.

Mains Castle

Mains consists of a six-storey tower house and two lower ranges, all arranged around a small, walled courtyard. Its otherwise relatively bijou footprint is multiplied manifold by the sheer visual power of the unusual tower, which dominates the landscape. The edifice was started by the Grahams of Fintry sometime between 1480 and 1500, when it may have been little more than a hunting lodge – the Grahams had their main house in the centre of Dundee. Mains Castle has a date stone marked 1562, the year David Graham and his wife Dame Margaret Ogilvy took up residence; the principal structure dates from this period. Thirty years later, David Graham was executed for taking part in a failed plot to re-establish Catholicism as the state religion. After a number of subsequent owners, the site was eventually abandoned in 1740, and, during the nineteenth century, was well known as a picturesque ruin. Sir James Caird bought and restored the castle in 1913, later handing it over, along with the park, to Dundee Council, who still own the site. In the later decades of the twentieth century, the castle became a crumbling eyesore and fell prey to vandals. It was eventually restored in 1988, later functioning as a restaurant. After several changes of tenant, it is no longer open to the public but is now a deservedly popular venue for weddings and corporate events.

The Murdered Lady

Mains Castle is one of the few medieval buildings left in Dundee, and as such has attracted what might be termed 'castle legends' – the kind of legends that cling to castles simply because such structures feed into our imagination. The earliest of these legends is a romantic ghost from the Middle Ages. Supposedly, a lady of the castle, caught in the act of infidelity, was murdered by her husband. Her ghostly tradition was imaginatively set down in *The Baronie of Hilltowne Dundee*, a 1927 book by the Revd William Skinner, minister of Hilltown United Free Church:

> She may now be seen, on a certain night of the month, when the moon is full and veering to the west, in her remorse, letting

down from the topmost window in the Tower her paramour with a rope round his neck, till with a great jerk he seems to fall into the earth; then she raises her hand in a sign of revulsion at the traitor's body below, and vanishes into the Tower.

Another record of the tradition was set out in verse, with suitable poetic licence, by Joseph Lee. In *Tales o' Our Town*, Lee tells us the whole story in his title and subtitle: 'The Castle of Mains. A Ballad of the Cruel and Jealous Murther by Gilchrist, Earl of Angus, of his Ladye, the Sister of King William the Lion of Scotland.'

Like many other traditional ghosts of the nineteenth century, the Murdered Lady of Mains exists only in hearsay, without a single recorded sighting. I suspect her legend begins on the printed page, and – as the result of the popularity of one particular book – became translated to folklore during the 1800s.

Unlike some of our other ghosts, she starts with an 'origin death', this death being found in a much celebrated (and denigrated) book of the sixteenth century – *Scotorum Historiae* (aka The History of the Scottish People) by Hector Boece. Boece (1465-1536) was a local lad from Dundee who went on to become the Principal of Aberdeen University. For generations his work was one of the few scholarly accounts of Scottish history, and was widely disseminated. But ever since Victorian historians started picking apart *Scotorum Historia*, and pointing out errors, inventions and fables, Boece's reputation has plummeted, and many researchers of the period now regard his work as little more than a collection of historical fantasies. One dissenting voice is Dana F. Sutton from the University of California. His analysis can be found on the online site The Philological Museum (www.philological.bham.ac.uk/), which disseminates Renaissance and Reformation Humanist writings under the auspices of the Shakespeare Institute of the University of Birmingham.

Sutton's argument is that, in Boece's time, the writing of history was not meant to be accurate but to be didactic. That is, it was designed to demonstrate the superiority of certain moral values, or eternal truths, for the instruction of the young men of the educated elite. As Boece was writing for the educated elite in a Scotland governed by Stuart kings, his work is shot through with exaggerated Scottish patriotic triumphs that show the Stuarts in a kindly light, while traducing their historical enemies or rivals (such as, for example, Macbeth). What all this comes down to is that Boece was not writing a Scottish history, but a contemporary mythology of Scotland. He was inventing Scotland not as it was, but as it should have been – at least, how it should have been from the point of view of the Stuarts and their supporters.

This mythology was profoundly influential – and continues to be so. The Scottish Humanist scholar, George Buchanan (1506-1582), who wrote a *History of Scotland*, is greatly indebted to Boece. Buchanan, in turn, influenced the English writer Raphael Holinshed (1529-1580), whose *Chronicles* gave William Shakespeare much of the material for his historical plays (including the entirely inaccurate portrait of Macbeth). Buchanan's history was very popular in the nineteenth century, and many Victorian Scots, interested in their nation's heritage, would have had a copy on their shelves. And within its pages, taken entirely from Boece, was the story of how Gilchrist murdered his unfaithful wife. This is what the original source, Hector Boece, wrote:

Earl Gillechrist of Angus, who had married the king's sister as a reward for the outstanding martial virtue he had often displayed at many places ... was enraged because he suspected his wife of adultery. He first ejected her from his castle, and then hanged her at Mannes, a village about a mile from Dundee. The king was very irate at the indignity of the thing (for she was his sister), and stripped him of all his goods.

The Scottish King William I, known as William the Lion (1165-1214), was troubled with insurrection in Galloway throughout his reign, and several times Gilchrist, the 3rd Earl of Angus, is recorded as having being dispatched to the south-west of the country to smite the rebels. As the king's strong right arm, and as a rich and powerful aristocrat to boot, Gilchrist was a suitable dynastic match for William's sister. There is only one problem with the story: did he actually marry her?

The records for the period are confusing and incomplete, and often contradict each other. Gilchrist seems to have been born around 1160, and died in his late forties between 1207 and 1211. Some genealogical authorities (such as James Taylor's *The Great Historic Families of Scotland*) state that he married one of William's sisters. Others doubt whether the wedding ever took place. *The Complete Peerage*, for example, states: 'It has been said, but it is doubtful, that his wife was Maud, or Marjory, sister of King William the Lion.' Further genealogies show Gilchrist's successive wives as Ingibiorg Ericksdottir and Margary Haroldsdottir, both the daughters of Scandinavian aristocrats from Orkney. Neither Boece nor Buchanan give the name of the king's murdered sister, so it is possible that Margary Haroldsdottir may have become mixed up with 'Marjory, sister of King William the Lion.' Unfortunately, there is no solid documentary evidence that William even had a sister named Marjory. The only 'evidence' which proves that Gilchrist and an unnamed king's sister were wed lies in the dubious pages of Hector Boece.

If the connection between the ghost and Gilchrist is tenuous, so is the link with Mains. In Boece's passage Mannes is clearly Mains, but there is nothing in the extract that tells us where the earl's castle was actually located. Indeed, no trace of any earlier structure has been found at Mains, and, situated as it is in a lea below a table of higher ground, the Den o'Mains was no place to build a defensive castle during the turbulent twelfth century. If Gilchrist did have a castle in the Strathdichty area, no record of it survives; but it was certainly not at Mains.

So, we have an alleged ghost of a murder victim with nothing more than a very dubious historical connection to the supposed events, and no genuine association with the site at Mains. Also, although the ghost is described in great detail (in some versions she lowers her escaping lover on a rope and then puts her hand to her throat as if to ward off strangulation), there is no record of anyone actually witnessing the apparition. Therefore, I have no hesitation in stating that this particular ghost is a romantic fancy of someone who had read the story in Buchanan's history, and with dramatic flair invented the repeating apparition of the murdered princess.

Modern Phenomena

Recently, there have been a number of much more interesting reports, which suggest that some kind of low-level haunting-type phenomena is present within the castle. The evidence comes from two sources: a visit to Mains by the paranormal research group Ghost Finders Scotland on 15 March 2008, the full details of which can be found on their website www.ghostfinders.co.uk; and the personal communications of Victor and Elena Peterson, who have been tenants at the castle since August 2007. (Victor, by the way, told me that he used to play in the castle, its derelict magnificence an irresistible magnet for the local boys, all of whom knew it was 'haunted'.)

The principal structures within the castle are the conjoined tower and north range, both of which are reached by the spiral staircase within the tower. The ground-floor entrance in the tower leads directly to the staircase, with a side door off to a modern kitchen running beneath the north range – this was once a set of cellars. Ascending the stairs, you are taken directly into the main hall with its adjacent bar, both within the north range. The ancient fabric of the castle is evident all around here – the bar, for example, has a colossal fireplace and the remnants of a corner turret staircase – and, not surprisingly, the high-ceilinged main hall is a popular venue for wedding banquets. Returning to the tower staircase, the next spiral – complete with a grotesque carved Green Man figure – brings you to the function room in the north range, directly above the main hall. Wedding ceremonies take place here if the weather is too inclement for a ceremony within the courtyard. The atmosphere of this room is less impressive than the main hall, largely because the ceiling is lower and much of it is covered in modern wood panelling. An original door leads to another bar, again wood panelled, with a further remnant of the corner tower, plus an original fireplace. This is the top floor of the north range.

The main hall at Mains Castle, set out for a wedding reception. (The Author)

Within the gloomy, ghostly place,
Then do I sit me down to trace
A stony, staring, Gorgon face
That glow'rs from off the stairway wall
From 'The Castle of Mains' by Joseph Lee.
(Ségolène Dupuy)

In 2007, Victor Peterson, having just moved in, was working late in the main hall, renewing the floorboards. A person not usually given to flights of imagination, he had a powerful sense that someone or something was behind him. He couldn't see or hear anything when he turned round, but he was convinced that the sensation was real.

During the 2008 investigation, members of the Ghost Finders' team recorded inexplicable temperature fluctuations, with the temperature seeming to change in response to one of the team; whatever was present seemed to cool the room down upon request.

During the same session, what sounded like people talking at a distance was detected, while a woman's voice was clearly heard on two separate occasions. In each case the sounds were witnessed by more than one team member, and a check showed that the castle was empty except for the investigation team, with all external doors locked.

Sometime in 2009, Elena Peterson was in the main hall with a client, going through the arrangements for a wedding booking. As they wandered round, both she and the guest heard what sounded like furni-

The upper room in the tower, with the roof-beams. (The Author)

The first two upper-storey single rooms in the tower are relatively small, while the topmost is much larger and airier, as here the tower expands into a square, overhanging attic, with the stair entering through the floor. This uppermost space is dominated by the cross-beams supporting the roof. During the 2008 visit, the group's medium became so uncomfortable in this room – apparently picking up an aura of medieval black magic – that she had to bolt back down the narrow spiral staircase.

With no apparitions, no moving objects and no visual phenomena, it may seem that these experiences are relatively minor. And perhaps they are, but that is what makes them so intriguing. Of course, it is possible that some of the sounds have a mundane origin. There are no trees near enough to the castle to brush along the roof, but perhaps birds or rats are active in an attic space, or possibly pesky kids occasionally manage to climb onto the roof of the north range. It is conceivable that some configuration within the castle's rooms and staircase transmits and amplifies voices from one part of the structure to another. And perhaps, as with Victor Peterson's imaginative childhood adventures, the simple 'castle-ness' of the structure brings to mind Gothic fancies. Certainly, on a foggy night, the way the tower looms out of the dark can be quite creepy. Yet, the subtle, low-key nature of the reported phenomena suggests that, just perhaps, something might be going on at Mains.

ture being dragged across bare floorboards in the function room above. Three factors are of interest here: firstly, no one else was present anywhere in the castle; secondly, the function room is entirely carpeted, with not a bare floorboard to be seen; and thirdly, a very similar experience was recorded during the 2008 investigation. Back in the tower, and through a locked door, each turn upwards on the now much narrower spiral staircase reveals a single room on each of the three subsequent tower storeys. The Ghost Finders' team had assembled in the second of these rooms; when everyone was present, they heard loud noises akin to furniture being dragged across a wooden floor. These noises were heard seven times over a short period, and were interspersed with what sounded like running footsteps on a wooden floor.

five

Spooky Ships – Discovery and the Frigate Unicorn

DUNDEE is fortunate in having two historic ships open to the public: the Royal Research Ship *Discovery* and the Royal Navy Frigate HMS *Unicorn*. The former, a three-masted vessel based on the design of a Dundee whaler, sits in a custom-built dock next to a visitor centre, while the *Unicorn*, the most complete ship of its class still afloat, lies in Victoria Dock, less than a mile to the east. Both are reputedly haunted, but, this aside, each ship is well worth a visit, being rich in period atmosphere, and a tangible link with adventure on the high seas.

RRS *DISCOVERY*

Discovery famously took Captain Robert Falcon Scott and his crew on their great voyage of exploration to Antarctica in 1901. It was the world's first ship specifically dedicated to scientific research, and carried on-board the technology for a number of experiments. The voyage greatly increased our knowledge of, among other things, zoology, oceanography, geography, ecology, atmospheric phenomena and the Earth's magnetic field. The ship became stuck in the ice for more than two years, eventually being rescued by the relief vessel *Terra Nova*, with the crew finally coming home to a hero's welcome in 1904. Scott returned to the Antarctic on the *Terra Nova* in 1910; but, in February 1912, he and Captain Lawrence Oates, Dr Edward Wilson, Lieutenant Henry Bowers, and Petty Officer Edgar Evans all perished during the expedition to the South Pole, memorably described as being 'the worst journey in the world'.

The Royal Research Ship Discovery. *(The Author)*

Discovery *through a porthole. (The Author)*

Following Scott's first expedition, *Discovery* had an eventful life, being used as a munitions ship in the First World War. She took part in two further scientific expeditions to Antarctica, before finally becoming a training ship for the Sea Scouts and the Royal Navy Reserve in the south of England. Scott's expedition dominates the contemporary *Discovery* narrative, but the ship saw several further decades of action, with hundreds of men journeying on her for a variety of purposes – a factor which is sometimes forgotten when trying to match the 'ghosts' to history. On 3 April 1986, *Discovery* returned to Dundee, the port where she was constructed, and after restoration became the star attraction at the superb Discovery Point visitor centre. The ship itself projects a potent presence, filled with sails and ropes, maritime paraphernalia, cramped cabins, narrow passageways and low-ceilinged spaces below decks.

In terms of haunting phenomena, the most common feature is the sound of anomalous footsteps. These have been heard for a number of years – in his 1998 book *Haunted Scotland*, Norman Adams reported that, when *Discovery* was in Dundee's Victoria Dock, before being towed to its present position, both the night watchman and a former ship's manager heard the loud footsteps. In 2001,

visitors' guide Robert Conway told Dane Love (author of *Scottish Spectres*) that other volunteers had heard footsteps on otherwise empty decks. Loud bangs have also been heard. Anecdotal evidence over the past decade has gradually built up and the present night watchman, Ed Feeney, has stated that he and other members of staff have heard the footsteps. I add my own two penn'orth here; in August 2010, myself and several other members of the Ghost Club were sitting in the wardroom when we all heard several loud footsteps on the empty deck above, proceeding from the stern end of the ship in the direction of the bow.

At present, the footsteps remain unexplained, although subsequent investigation has shown that sounds made in one part of the ship appear unexpectedly loud in other, unrelated areas. So, the footsteps may be paranormal, or they could be created by some hitherto unsuspected aspect of the physical environment of the century-old vessel.

Also fairly common on the *Discovery*'s haunting checklist is the phenomenon of a 'sense of presence' or feeling of unease. Guide Robert Conway, for example, told Dane Love that some visitors reported a 'bad feeling' in the wardroom, the social area for the officers. Most of the evidence for this 'sense of presence' is anecdotal, without full descriptions, dates or named witnesses, but one occasion has been formally recorded. A statement on the website of the Dundee & Angus Convention Bureau states that:

> During one large conference held at Discovery Point and on-board the *Discovery,* staff had to move the break out session on the ship after a guest refused to go into the Coal Bunker because she felt a ghostly presence.

On board Discovery *at night. (The Author)*

The wardroom on Discovery, *location of many strange experiences. (The Author)*

A spokesperson for Dundee Heritage Trust was quoted as saying:

> This wasn't the first time that we've had guests experience paranormal activities. The woman was really reluctant to go into the Coal Bunker so we closed the auditorium which forms part of the exhibition and hosted the break out session there instead.

'Sense of presence' is one of the more commonly reported paranormal phenomena, and because of its very nature is frustratingly elusive to investigate. There is a school of thought among some researchers that it may be caused by a mix of human psychology and environmental factors. As visitors quickly discover, the vessel's internal spaces are cramped and rarely lit by daylight, and this can give rise to a mild feeling of claustrophobia which can in turn engender notions of 'eerieness'. In addition, it has been found that infrasound – soundwaves below the level of human hearing – can create false sensations of paranormal activity. Infrasound is often generated in tubes or shafts, and it is possible that some of the complex narrow spaces within the ship may act in this way. On the other hand, no one has yet attempted to record any possible infrasound aboard, and the various reports of a sense of presence have not been catalogued and matched to any potential environmental causes. So, in the case of this particular phenomenon, we have next-to-no data; once again, this could be genuinely paranormal, or it could be another factor influenced by the *Discovery*'s physical status.

Then there is the case of the imploding light bulb. The bulb in one of the officer cabins off the wardroom kept blowing, for no obvious electrical reason. There are also anecdotal reports of snoring being heard from this cabin. On the 1901 voyage to Antarctica, the bunk was occupied by Ernest Shackleton, which has given rise to the belief that the famous explorer still haunts the ship – and several published and online works on the paranormal claim that Shackleton perished while on the *Discovery*. In fact, Shackleton died onboard the Norwegian whaler *Quest*, during his 1921-22 expedition to Antarctica; he is buried on the sub-Antarctic island of South Georgia. I suspect that Shackleton, one of the great British heroes of the Edwardian age and a truly formidable individual, is identified as the source of the electrical and audio anomalies simply because he is so well known. The cabin must have been used by dozens of sailors and officers over the decades, but when speculating on the identity of the 'ghost', Shackleton's fame trumps these less-celebrated men, distorting any attempt to accurately analyse the phenomena. It's the paranormal equivalent of contemporary celebrity culture.

The final phenomenon – the sighting of an apparent apparition – has only one recorded example. *Scottish Spectres* relates the episode of a visitor in the late 1990s greeting 'the man in the corner'. The tourist apparently spent some time chatting to the figure, which was invisible to the guide and everyone else.

Wherever there is a haunting, people tend to look for the 'origin story', the death or deaths that supposedly 'explain' the phenomena. But ghosts are elusive, and rarely provide any kind of clue as to their identity. Linking reports of deaths to reports of ghosts is something done by the living – simply because we like clear story arcs, so that we can provide a satisfying link between that death and this haunting, tying the whole thing up in a neat narrative package. Sadly for such attempts, ghosts are

Ernest Shackleton. (From E. H. Shackleton, The Heart of the Antarctic, 1909)

Shackleton's cabin, supposedly haunted by the adventurer. (The Author)

rarely co-operative in the construction of these stories.

For example, the usual 'origin death' at the source of the *Discovery's* alleged haunting is ascribed to Charles Bonner, a young Able Seaman who died on 21 December 1901. He fell to his death from the crow's nest when the ship was in New Zealand, stocking up for the last stage of the trip to the Antarctic continent. The place on the main deck where his body hit, below the main mast, is sometimes said, without real justification, to be the focus of the haunting. Far less celebrated in the supernatural annals is Able Seaman George Vince, who died in McMurdo Sound, Antarctica in 1902. He slid over the edge of a cliff, his body never being found. Vince's death lacks the sheer on-board drama of Bonner's, and so he does not feature in the usual narrative when the story of the *Discovery* ghost is being told.

Further, we have no idea whether anyone else died on-board between 1904 and the mid-twentieth century.

Sadly for any attempt to find an authentic link between the recorded phenomena and real people and their lives or deaths, there is nothing to go on. The footsteps, noises, electrical issues and the alleged apparition are entirely devoid of personality – and so we cannot associate them with Ernest Shackleton, Charles Bonner, or any other historical figure.

HMS *UNICORN*

From the outside, HMS Frigate *Unicorn* is initially less impressive than *Discovery* because it has been stripped of its masts and sails, and its top deck has been roofed over, giving it the impression of a ship that

HMS *Frigate* Unicorn *at Victoria Dock.* (The Author)

has been mothballed. This is actually what happened, as the post-Napoleonic 'peace dividend' meant that the warship was not needed when it was first launched, and then it was made redundant by the new-fangled steam ships. Over the decades, *Unicorn* functioned as a powder store on the Thames, then from 1873 moved to Dundee as a drill ship for training and a Royal Naval Volunteer Reserve administrative HQ. This may not sound an exciting prospect but, once inside, you discover this is another wonderful vessel to explore – it is, in fact, the oldest British naval ship still afloat. It bears many of the original warfare features from its launch in 1824: including cannon, hammocks, mess area, officers' wardroom and captain's cabin, complete with removable doors for ease of movement during the height of action. Short of visiting HMS *Victory* in Portsmouth, this is almost the closest you will get to a warship of the 'golden age of sail', when the Royal

Navy ruled the waves. It is also, it should be said, filled with dark, low, claustrophobic compartments, so the same psychological caveats about the *Discovery*'s 'environment of anxiety' also apply here. And, of course, one should bear in mind that this is an old wooden vessel, prone to groaning and banging with the weather and temperature, while the sound of footsteps and creaking floorboards can travel from one part of the ship to another.

Like the *Discovery*, HMS *Unicorn* has a minor history of spookiness. It has been investigated four times by paranormal groups: on 18 November 2006 by Paranormal Discovery (in a joint investigation with Spiritfinders Scotland); on 7 April 2007 by Ghost Finders Scotland; and on 20 October 2007 and 8 May 2008 by Paranormal Discovery again. The later date was a charity event organised by radio station Wave 102, with members of the public taking part alongside the investigators.

The nature of the charity event meant that incident recording and confirmation procedures were 'looser' than during a more organised investigation. The full reports can be found on the groups' respective websites.

Being a warship, the *Unicorn* is both larger than and structured differently from the *Discovery*, the upper decks generally being much more open plan. The easiest way to discuss the alleged paranormal activity is to go through the ship deck-by-deck, starting with the uppermost section.

The Forecastle and Quarterdeck

In most ships, this would be the deck open to the elements, but as *Unicorn* was relegated to a 'reserve' function and stored, here you are entirely enclosed under a wooden roof. This is the only remaining example of this once-common method of preserving ships, and also the reason why all the fittings are in such good condition. A number of the smaller cannon are kept on this deck.

The Quarterdeck is the site of one of the most dramatic incidents, which took place in the mid-2000s. Ship Manager Bob Hovell was going about his business as he did every day when, from near the ship's wheel, he saw a male figure briefly move across the deck. No one else was in the area at the time, and from an examination of the deck and the surrounding area it is difficult to see how a shadow or reflection could have been

The location on the Unicorn's Quarterdeck where the Ship Manager saw an apparition. (The Author)

projected into the space. In the evenings, car headlights and other light sources intrude through the Quarterdeck windows, but Bob's sighting occurred in broad daylight, around about noon on a cloudy Sunday. At the time, Bob put it down to overwork and fatigue, and although he knows that he saw the apparent apparition, he is ambivalent about its reality.

The Gun Deck

The Gun Deck is the business end of the frigate, with a panoply of heavy cannon, as well as the captain's cabin. It is the first deck visitors arrive on, and also contains Bob Hovell's small reception area and shop counter. Bob recalls that a display bookcase in this area was found thrown onto the floor, at a time when no one was aboard. During the November 2006 investigation, one of the female members of the Paranormal Discovery team felt as if an invisible hand had touched or tickled the top of her head. This took place in the captain's cabin. A feeling of being touched was something that visitors had previously reported to Bob.

The Mess Deck (aka the Lower Deck)

This is the lowest deck many visitors get to, as the Orlop Deck below can be tricky to access. The Mess Deck has no windows, is low-ceilinged and is steeped in shadows – hence can seem 'creepy'. Here one can find the officers' cabins and wardroom, and the crewmen's hammocks and eating tables.

During the April 2007 investigation, several members of the Ghost Finders' team witnessed one hammock swaying while its companion remained perfectly still. The evening weather was placid, with no wind, and no obvious movement of the ship. One team member heard twelve loud footsteps on the Gun Deck above, followed by a

The Carpenter's Walk in the Orlop Deck of the frigate. (The Author)

The Orlop Deck

This is the 'cellar' in the very bowels of the ship, being not so much a deck as a series of platforms, powder magazines and storage holds. A low, back-breaking walkway known as the Carpenter's Walk runs along one side, connecting some of the areas. The Orlop Deck is below the waterline, and its dim and congested spaces can create a sense of disorientation and discomfort.

The April 2007 visit by Ghost Finders Scotland recorded a series of phenomena down here: temporary battery drainage, speedily reversed; temporary equipment failure; a strong smell of woodsmoke; a loud crack, following a request for any spirits present to make themselves known through sound; and other bangs and noises. One investigator felt a slap on the back of her neck, followed by a gentle kick. Another reported the sensation of a hand on her cheek, and a third felt something hit his back, as if a small object had been thrown at him. In May 2008, one of the guests at the charity event reported seeing a standing figure, but no one else in the group witnessed anything.

My suspicions are immediately aroused by the fact that the most self-evidently eerie part of the ship – the Orlop Deck – is the very area where the majority of phenomena have been reported; I wonder whether environmental and psychological issues are at play here. On the other hand, the range and variety of the other phenomena, although low-level, is intriguing. Some may have their origin in the physical nature of a wooden ship that is almost two centuries old; others may arise from expectation, exaggeration and wish-fulfilment. But perhaps, just perhaps, there is something supernatural lurking within this magnificent museum piece.

bang or thud, as if someone had put down a heavy object. Investigation showed that the Gun Deck was empty and all the doors were locked. Other bangs were also heard on the Mess Deck, but the ship's acoustic geography made it difficult to identify where the noises occurred and what had caused them.

During the charity event, several members of the public in attendance stated that they had seen shadows moving in front of the doorway to the wardroom. More movements were reported when sitting in the wardroom and looking back into the mess area. Three guests saw a bright light by the stairwell. There was an upsurge of a phenomenon common to paranormal investigations – temporary unexplained equipment failure, in this case affecting a fully-charged video camera. An investigator felt a light push on her back as she stood in front of one of the cabins, and two further figures were later glimpsed, one sitting down on a floor grille and the other just a pair of legs wearing blue trousers.

In May 2011, Bob Hovell told me that, among the fairly common experiences reported by visitors (uncomfortable feelings, eeriness and so on), a small boy a few weeks previously had said that he saw a lot of faces on the lower decks but that they were all dead.

six

Fakes, Frauds & Folklore – and Spring-Heeled Jack!

THE newspapers of nineteenth-century Dundee are a rich source of ghost stories – but usually of a kind where the 'ghost' is identifiably human, mortal, and being a nuisance. Sometimes the reports are an exercise in frustration, with key details omitted from the descriptions, and an almost complete absence of follow-up stories. Not everything in them can be taken at face value, and so period newspaper reports, fascinating though they may be, often end up telling us far less than we would like to know, especially when it comes to fake phantoms.

Perhaps the first of the fakes dated to some time in the 1820s. In *Reminiscences of an Old Dundonian*, published in 1882, septuagenarian J.M. Beatts looked back on his childhood and early manhood, recalling a 'ghost' who was said to haunt the Hilltown every night, dressed all in white but with a black face. Captain Downie, one of first superintendents during the early days of the police force, ambushed the figure and chased it towards Rosebank, eventually downing his quarry with a cudgel. The 'spectre' turned out to be a tall black man, who went under the name of the Black Doctor. He was charged with 'alarming the lieges',

an early version of breach of the peace, and was released on the equivalent of bail. He promptly skipped town, abandoning the money he had handed over for his pledge.

A classic case of a rumoured haunting appeared in the *Courier* on 29 December 1852. The headline read: 'A GHOST IN THE MURRAYGATE'; the story related the events with brusque efficiency:

> For several evenings in succession last week, large crowds of silly people were to be seen gazing at an empty house in the Murraygate, attracted by the report that it was haunted by a veritable Ghost. The report having reached the ears of the police, an examination of the premises took place. Nothing was discovered to shew the presence of an inhabitant of the other world, other than the accidental blowing out of the candle carried by one of the officers caused by the opening of a door, which was set down by the terrified onlookers outside to the credit of the ghost. We understand, however, that sufficient evidence was found to shew that scenes of revelry had recently been enacted in the house; and there is little doubt that the noise made by those who

Looking through to Seagate from Murraygate. From Lamb's Dundee: Its Quaint & Historic Buildings. *(Perth & Kinross Libraries)*

The steeply-sloping Logie Kirkyard on Lochee Road. (The Author)

had thus lawlessly taken possession of the premises led to the report of a ghost.

'A GHOST IN LOGIE KIRKYARD – INTREPID CONDUCT OF A POLICEMAN.'

This was the enticing headline for a long piece in the *Courier* on 22 June 1869. The events described had taken place around ten days previously, during the 'white nights' of midsummer – when only a few hours of darkness interrupted the long summer daylight. Just before midnight, the local constable was pacing his beat when he saw a strange figure in the midst of Logie Kirkyard. The burial ground occupies a small but prominent hillock right next to the road, so that someone walking on the pavement can easily see over the wall and up the slopes of the gravestone-bedecked mound.

One excited journalist wrote:

> The sight of the figure was indeed enough to appal the stoutest heart, it was some six feet high, straight as a pole, and completely arrayed in white. It moved slowly and majestically forward amongst the tall rank grass surrounding the gravestones, and when the silence of the place and the lateness of the hour are taken into account, the constable, when his eyes first lighted on the strange apparition, might have been excused had he beaten a retreat.

The copper, however, had noticed that the figure had just thrown a stone at him, and so, with lantern in hand and threats voiced, he was about to climb over the wall to apprehend the apparition when a well-heeled lady and gentleman came up; the former was thrown into cries and screams at the sight of the white-robed figure. After spending some time calming the woman, the constable again ventured into the grave-yard, this time accompanied by the lady's husband. Sadly, however, the ghost moved off to the rear of the cemetery as the two men were making their way up the slope, and disappeared in the shadows. Nothing more was discovered. 'We leave our readers,' the *Courier* concluded, 'to conjecture whether the disguise was doffed, and the ghost found refuge in some of the adjacent houses, or that, its "leave" having expired, the earth opened, and it was swallowed up.'

Phantoms returned to the *Courier* on 17 November 1873, under the misleading title of 'A LOCHEE GHOST STORY'. Starting off with a statement of apparent veracity: 'A correspondent sends us the following, for the truth of which he vouches', the story describes the experiences of a pair of sweethearts, one of whom was from Lochee, who were walking back from a ball in the early hours of the morning when they decided to call in on the girl's parents. As the family lived close to Liff church, the couple took a short cut through the graveyard, which is a large flat area in the centre of the village, curving around the parish kirk, which was built on the site of a much older church in 1839. Then, as the paper reported, things got weird:

> They had only got the length of the churchyard when they were confronted by a most ghastly spectacle, in the shape of a figure like one of the 'sheeted dead', which stood before them in the road, holding a lighted candle in the one hand, while the other grasped a long pole.

The girl screamed and her lover was struck speechless, but, being a well-brought-up young man, he gathered his wits and politely addressed the figure with: 'This is a fine night, sir.' The spectre responded with just a squeak – which doesn't sound very

The church and cemetery at Liff. (The Author)

spectral – but then apparently began to change shape:

> The figure gradually began to assume larger proportions, and ultimately raised itself some twelve feet in the air, came down with a terrific force that shook the ground, and in a twinkling the light disappeared and so did the ghost.

This climactic event caused the young lady to swoon, and so her beau carried her to her parents' house, where she soon recovered.

As with so many of these newspaper reports, the Liff episode raises more questions than it can answer. Ostensibly another example of the by-now-standard jape of dressing up in a white sheet and flitting about a graveyard, it has some anomalous elements. Liff village was then a very small place, and the chances of pedestrians wandering through the graveyard in the early hours would have been very slim – so why would someone be waiting during a cold November night with sheet, pole and candle, just on the off-chance that a victim would happen by? And what was all that business about the spirit growing in size, rising off the ground, and returning with a crash? Was this in fact not a fake phantom but a genuine supernatural event?

My cynical suspicions are that – assuming the event is even partly authentic – it was some kind of set-up. Perhaps an acquaintance of the couple left the ball before them and decided to waylay them for a prank. Or perhaps either the girl or the lad arranged the event in advance, as part of a covert romantic gambit designed to bring the couple closer together, both emotionally and physically. As for the ghost's expansion and levitation, I suggest this was exaggeration or invention. Of course, I could be wrong and perhaps the young couple had indeed encountered something supernatural that night – but I'm betting it was a human companion, in a sheet, performing a pre-arranged charade.

Another fake ghost concerned with affairs of the heart appeared in the *Courier* on 12 March 1886, under the heading: 'A STRANGE VISITOR AT A WEDDING.' Sadly no location was given, other than 'a quiet little burgh on the south-western confines of the county of Angus.' The occasion was the wedding between a man in his seventies and 'a buxom widow, fully thirty years his junior'. The septuagenarian had lost his wife of fifty years just a few months earlier, and local feeling was running high – basically, the local busybodies were pontificating that remarrying so quickly was nothing less than a moral outrage and a total disgrace. As a result, a crowd of some 200 decided to hang around outside the house where the marriage party was being celebrated, and two constables had to be present to ensure no disturbance took place. As a further precaution, the outside door was locked.

Inside, the attendees numbered no more than seven or eight in total. Things were progressing smoothly when, according to the newspaper, 'a ghastly-looking figure, clothed in white … glided into the room, to the consternation of all present.' The figure offered to shake hands with some of the women present (who responded with screams of shock) and then identified herself as the bridegroom's recently deceased spouse. She went up to the old man and demanded from him the money she had scrimped to save over the years, and which he was now lavishing on his new bride. The figure then quietly withdrew with a final enigmatic comment, that she would come again.

Although obviously some kind of ploy to disrupt the unpopular marriage, the 'lady in white' arrived and departed without hindrance, plied her task in the presence of the minister, and left behind a village seething with gossip, which eventually made it, in attenuated form, into the columns of the *Courier*. But, as with many similar episodes, this was its only appearance in print and we are given no idea as to what happened next.

It's Spring-Heeled Jack!

The early months of 1883 saw a kind of panic, with considerable column inches given over to describe the antics of a phantom menace causing a nuisance in the city. The *Courier* kicked things off on 16 January with an article headlined: 'THE GHOST OF BLACKNESS QUARRY – A BLACK APPARITION IN DUNDEE.' 'For some weeks past,' the article stated, 'people living in the neighbourhood of Blackness Quarry have been kept in a feverish state of alarm by the erratic movements of a nocturnal apparition, haunting the quarry and the adjacent lanes leading to it from the Hawkhill.' The locus of the apparition was the old quarry next to Blackness Road, by then abandoned and partially occupied by stables and wood yards. Described as 'a dreary, gruesome region', it was unlit and had multiple access routes from Blackness Road, Bellfield Lane and Louden's Alley, thus making surreptitious entry and exit all too easy. The 'spectre' was described as a 'big black man enveloped from neck to heel with a dark cloak or topcoat. His head was covered with a broad slouched hat, pulled well down to conceal his face.'

The silent figure, who was sometimes seen patrolling the quarry around midnight with a handheld candle, first spooked children and a number of old women during December. The rumours amplified and spread quickly, and soon children were afraid to go outside at night, and housewives refused to go to wells for water or enter cellars for coals. The *Courier* described the working-class population of the vicinity as being in 'a state of chronic excitement', and it was clear that many at least half-believed the figure to be preternatural in origin. Very shortly, however, the supposed spectre was displaying more human attributes. On New Year's Eve, it followed a woman into her home and demanded to know if there was anything left to drink in the Hogmanay bottle. Then, one Sunday night, an unexplained gunshot was heard in the quarry. 'Matters reached a crisis on Saturday night week,' stated the paper, 'when a staid old couple coming home pretty late saw the "black spectre" standing grim and solitary in a dark lane.' The couple fled in terror and shut themselves up in their own house. The following night, an ex-policeman was told that the black man was in the lane, and rushed out armed with the kitchen poker, the sight of which sent the tall man in black fleeing into the darkness of the quarry. Inevitably, the panic brought about vigilantism, and a few nights later a mob cornered a gentleman in black clothes; the former policeman was summoned to identify the miscreant, but he stated that, 'the black man he charged with the poker was as big again as that chap.'

Three weeks later, on 6 February, the *Courier* was back on the case, with a long piece entitled: 'A "GHOST" AT LARGE IN DUNDEE – ALLEGED SERIOUS RESULTS.' The report on 16 January had initially created a ghost hunt:

> The publicity given in our columns to the matter was the means of drawing to the vicinity of the Blackness Quarry large crowds of young men, boys, and girls nightly for about a week, all eager to see his ghostship, for whom, judging from their demeanour, they intended a warm greeting.

However, the figure made no appearance. Then, at the end of February, reports started to come in that the phantom had moved from the west of Dundee to the northern and eastern areas of the city, having been sighted over a wide range from Lochee through Clepington to the Ferry Road, with incidents occurring from midnight to the pre-dawn period, including:

> A Broughty Ferry butcher, accosted on the Ferry Road by 'a figure clad in white' which then seemed to disappear straight through a stone wall.
> A scavenger emptying an ashpit in the northern part of the city felt a hand on his shoulder. Turning to see the figure, he scared it off by shouting at it.
> Appearances in Kemback Street and Craigie Street, just west of Baxter Park.
> Two sightings by one witness in North Wellington Street in Hilltown, on one occasion between one and two a.m.
> More sightings in a field to the north of Arbroath Road and on the farm of West Craigie.

> The figure appearing from behind a tree on the Arbroath Road so suddenly that a young lady out walking with her sweetheart semi-collapsed and had to be assisted home.
> An encounter in Lochee, where a young man asked the figure the time of day, and received a 'bovine roar' in reply, with the ghost then running off.
> Several servants and young boys and girls shocked by the sudden appearance of the figure in parts of the Maryfield district.
> An assault on a girl in Crescent Street, in which some of her clothes were destroyed.
> A young mill boy in the east end confined to bed with a series of fits after encountering the figure coming out of a close.

There were reports of half-a-dozen young men arming themselves with impromptu weapons and searching, unsuccessfully, for the perpetrator of these crimes. The paper also speculated that the individual was a well-to-do gentleman acting out a bet, or simply bent on 'mischievous folly', and added a detailed description of the phantom:

> The 'ghost' may be described as being rather tall, and is generally seen dressed in a long dark cloak, although occasionally he sometimes assumes a luminous appearance, supposed to be due to the inside of the cloak being lined with cloth dipped in phosphorus, and exposed to view. Several yards of crape are also suspended from his hat … throughout the east end of the town he is, from the rapidity of his movements, popularly termed 'Springheels'.

At this point, the details of the report both implicitly and explicitly tip us towards a digression into a mention of one of the most fascinating and enduring figures of British urban folklore: Spring-Heeled Jack.

A modern artist's impression of Spring-Heeled Jack. (Richard Svensson/Fortean Picture Library)

Jack first appeared in the environs of London in 1837/38; he was a mysterious figure dressed in outlandish garb who launched a series of public assaults on young women. What appears to have been a case of a genuine criminal engaged in nefarious acts, quickly became an early-Victorian urban legend, helped in part by reports of the truly bizarre costume and actions of the original perpetrator. He was said to have been equipped with talons (to shred clothes), dressed in a long dark cloak or an all-encompassing bodysuit, and possessed of a darkened or hideous visage – with the ability to breathe fire! As the legend expanded through copycat assaults and uncritical press reporting, Jack was said to be able to leap high walls in a single bound, bringing him the sobriquet Spring-Heeled. He was said to wear armour to make him bullet-proof, and to have burning-red eyes. He was sometimes called a ghost.

By the middle of Victoria's reign, Jack was no longer just a rather weird criminal, but a fully-fledged demonic bogeyman, a figure of folklore and fear who occupied a special place in the British urban imagination. He turned up in Peckham (1872), Sheffield (1873), Liverpool (1904) and Bradford (1926). In the 1860s, he was thought to haunt the streets of Old Aberdeen. In the 1930s, he was being hunted in Glasgow. In 1877, he plagued the huge British Army camp at Aldershot, the events being widely and breathlessly reported in the sensational and weekly tabloid-like magazine *the Illustrated Police News*. Whoever was responsible for the Dundee events of 1883 would have been more than familiar with the alleged appearance and *modus operandi* of Spring-Heeled Jack (it is, of course, possible that, given the amount of ground covered, there was more than one perpetrator in Dundee).

A number of elements in the Dundee case are congruent with previous Spring-Heeled Jack panics:

The assault on the girl in Crescent Street: several of Jack's early attacks, from the 1830s onwards, have him shredding or cutting the garments of his female victims.

The predominantly female nature of the victims: the Aldershot soldiers notwithstanding, most of the people 'Jack' chose to attack were women or girls.

The shock felt by the victims, sometimes requiring medical treatment: this again is a feature of earlier assaults, indicating that the figure was probably scarier-looking than the average footpad.

The description of the figure as being tall and as wearing a long black cloak, and contrary statements that he was sometimes seen all in white: some of Jack's feats have him dressed in white, as in a conventional sheeted ghost.

The belief that his cloak was lined with luminous phosphorus: the phosphorus idea was a popular one at the time, although actually creating a garment coated with the volatile substance would have been both utterly impractical and most foolhardy.

His ability to apparently vanish without a trace: as in the butcher's account of the white-garbed figure moving through a solid wall.

The notion that the perpetrator was a member of the upper classes, operating on a bet or a dare: this too was a common idea during the 1830s panic, and it has something to commend it – Jack's high-quality cloak and/or clothes would have been beyond the reach of ordinary people.

Lastly, of course, there is his turn of speed, with the name 'Springheels' coming to the fore. All in all, it seems that someone in Dundee had read about Spring-Heeled Jack, and had been inspired.

On Friday 9 February, the *Courier* had more on the mysterious figure. Headlined 'GHOSTS AT LOCHEE', the article showed that 'the theatre of his nefarious and despicable foolery' had now shifted almost entirely to the community on the north-western edge of Dundee. Amongst the many sightings claimed were a milk-delivery boy who was 'almost frightened out of his wits by a ghostly-looking figure coming across his path'; two women accosted by a 'tall individual wearing a loose-hanging garment and slouched hat' in woodland at the north-east of Lochee; and a workman on the road to the north of the Law, who encountered a figure wearing a light, waterproof overcoat, an ordinary cap, and a white muffler. In the latter case, the witness stated that: 'the appearance of the face was frightsome in the extreme.' All the events took place between 9 p.m. and midnight, in darkness. The article finished with a typical indication of the nature of the panic:

> The matter is certainly a serious one, and ought to be put down immediately, for the amount of excitement and fear in the minds of young people, and women folk especially, is undoubtedly great, many being afraid to go out alone after nightfall.

At a guess, and given the different and apparently cheaper clothing sported by the Lochee prankster, the individual concerned may have been someone entirely different to the perpetrator of the events in the north and east of the city over the previous weeks.

The panic came to a close a little over a week later. On 19 February 1883, the *Advertiser* published a report from the local court proceedings, entitled: 'A MIDNIGHT DISTURBER OF THE PEACE.' Here is the piece in full:

A respectable-looking man named William Anderson, described as a clerk, residing in South Ellen Street, was brought before Bailie Bradford at the Dundee Police Court on Saturday charged with a contravention of the General Police Act. The charge set forth that Anderson stood on the footway close to the railings in front of a dwelling-house in Nethergate for about a quarter of an hour early on Saturday morning, and at intervals did 'yell or bawl at the approach of passengers, to the annoyance of several passengers'. He pleaded guilty, and explained that he had met several friends, with whom he unfortunately took too much liquor. The police info was to the effect that about half-past twelve o'clock the prisoner seemed to be acting the part of a 'ghost'. He took up a position in a dark shade in front of some houses in the Nethergate, and on any person appearing he rushed out uttering the most hideous yells. Several persons, it is said, were frightened by his conduct. The Magistrate said he was sorry to see a respectable man like the prisoner before the Court on such a charge. He trusted this would be a warning to Anderson, and dismissed him.

The *Scotsman* carried a shorter version of the same story on the same day, under the title: 'DUNDEE – A GHOST SEIZED.'

It seems unlikely that drunken William Anderson, clumsily launching into idiotic shouting bouts at passers-by, was the same person responsible for the uncanny Spring-Heeled Jack/ghost incidents that had held the city in thrall over the previous month. Nevertheless, the attacks ceased, and this particular 'ghost' troubled the good citizens of Dundee no more. The identity of the prankster will probably remain a mystery forever.

Interestingly, there had been two earlier 'Spring-Heeled Jacks' in Angus. On 10 November 1865, the *Courier* reported on 'AN IMITATOR OF SPRINGHEELS' at Kirriemuir, where an unnamed individual in a sheet was overpowered by his intended victim. And on 23 September 1879, the same paper had the headline 'A FORFAR GHOST STORY', in which Alexander James Harrison Robertson was fined £1 for disorderly conduct. This case involved dressing in white clothes and a slouch hat, and pretending to be a ghost for, as Robertson said, 'A piece of fun – an innocent frolic.' When Robertson was first spotted, witnesses had cried out: 'Spring heels!'

A resurgence of Spring-Heeled Jack-ism was reported in the *Courier* on 18 February 1893:

> During the past week or two many wild rumours have been floating about Barnhill and Broughty Ferry as to the nocturnal appearance of an individual of the 'Spring-Heeled Jack' order. He seems to take special delight in terrifying the servant girls of Barnhill. Dressed in a long Ulster, he approaches his unsuspecting victims, and suddenly goes through a transformation in dress calculated to shake the nerves of any lonely pedestrian.

The exact nature of this 'transformation in dress' is unknown. However, it seems that this particular japester had received his comeuppance, as the report concluded:

> The other night the gentleman in question, who has been the subject of earnest search by some public-spirited residents, is reported to have been caught on the highway, and received a castigation which will put a stop to his adventures for a few evenings at least.

A strange article appeared in the *Courier* on 31 January 1891, entitled 'A GHOST AT INVERGOWRIE':

> A ghost has made its appearance at Invergowrie, and is causing much perturbation by the antics it is carrying on. This is not a sham but a real ghost. It can salaam to its victim, almost touching the ground, and then raise itself up ten or twelve feet. It has a bare skull, and burns a blue light in its mouth, emitting a sulphurous smell, and rattles its bones in such a way as to strike terror to the heart of its victim. But retribution is at hand. Fathers and mothers are vowing vengeance. Traps are being laid, and the ghost's heid is to be split. Disappear, Mr Ghost, while there is yet time.

This is a bit of a head-scratcher. In one sentence the unnamed correspondent states that the ghost is genuine, and gives an impressive list of its supernatural accomplishments. Then the piece suggests that the ghost is a fake, and that outraged parents are planning to catch and punish the malefactor. I suspect this is a highly coded communiqué to the inhabitants of Invergowrie regarding some recent events, couched in abstract terms but full of meaning to those in the know. Perhaps there had been a series of pranks, or a teenage incident, or some kind of neighbourhood dispute. Whatever it meant, however, the 'ghost' did not trouble the pages of the *Courier* again, and so we are left entirely ignorant about what was really going on.

By now, it seems, fake phantoms were all the rage. On 14 and 15 November 1898, the *Courier* carried two related articles with the headlines, 'A DUNDEE GHOST – SENSATIONAL ADVENTURES IN THE WEST END' and 'THE DUNDEE "GHOST" – A SERIES OF ADVENTURES – A LAMPLIGHTER'S AMUSING EXPERIENCE'. Over the previous week, someone had been seen in the affluent western part of the city, mooning about enveloped in a white sheet. On the Thursday evening, the figure frightened a gardener, who fled but soon returned with his employer. The bellicose attitude of the latter caused the 'ghost' to turn tail and leap over a wall to hide in an adjacent garden.

Later reports came in from Binrock and the grounds of Farringdon Hall, both in the West End. Then the sheeted one appeared nearer the city centre. As the *Courier* condescendingly described it:

> A most amusing incident took place to the discomfiture of a worthy lamplighter. This servant of the municipality was in the performance of his duty passing the foot of Thomson Street, when he says he suddenly descried the white-robed figure standing by the side of a lamppost. His courage deserted him, and for a moment he stood breathless, but realising in a very few minutes that he was confronted only by flesh and blood he assumed a threatening attitude, and determined to use his stick on this midnight marauder. But the figure did not apparently wish to come to closer quarters. In fact, on the lamplighter making a move the man in white did ditto with considerably more agility. The lamplighter now opines that he saw a cloven hoof turning the corner of the street and disappearing in the mist; but considering discretion the better part of valour he made no effort to follow.

Some days earlier, the man-in-a-white-sheet had scared a young gardener's assistant named Macdonald at Clarendon Park Nurseries. A few evenings later the figure was seen again, standing motionless in the same spot among trees beside a footpath. This time Mr Grossart, the proprietor, gave chase, accompanied by a Mr Beats, young Macdonald, and another youth, with the parties splitting up and coming at the spectre from two different directions. The pursuit proceeded through a thicket running down the side of the wall between the nurseries and the neighbouring estate of Binrock, with the ghost negotiating the route in a way that showed he was a local man familiar with the intricacies of the path. Here the exciting chase reached its conclusion, as described in the *Courier*:

> Arrived at the wall, the man in white leaped over it in the Spring-heel Jack style. On reaching that part of the road midway between the wall and Binrock Lodge, the frightened visitor leapt as if to clear an obstacle in the shape of a barbed wire. Thereafter the apparition redoubled the speed at which it was proceeding, and soon left Mr Grossart, Mr Beats, and the boys behind.

No more was heard of the West End phantom after the report of 15 November, so presumably the individual concerned decided to hang up his sheet.

The final example of our historic hoaxes was reported in the *Courier* on 6 December 1900, under the heading 'THE PERTHSHIRE GHOST STORY – A CURIOUS HOAX':

> For some time past East Perthshire has been in a state of alarm over the appearance of an alleged ghost, said to be a son of a Dundee gentleman, who for a wager of £1,000 had undertaken to make a tour

through Perthshire adorned as one from the nether regions.

The spectre first appeared in Longforgan, moving on to Meigle, Alyth and Blairgowrie, and soon a wave of rumour, conjecture and misidentification was abroad, as described in the typical newspaper style of the period:

> Some alarm was caused in Perth yesterday by a report that two young ladies while going home from the theatre last night met the ghost in Bridgend. The only description they can give is that the ghost is a horrible looking man. They could not tell whether he had horns or not, but on being questioned they began to think he had. The young ladies had seen some paragraphs in the papers about the Blairgowrie ghost, and no doubt their imaginations were overwrought.

The identity of the alleged 'son of a Dundee gentleman' was never revealed, although the pool of suspects must have been small, as the bet of £1,000 in 1900 is the equivalent of over £50,000 today.

seven

'Traditional' Ghosts

IN this chapter we look at several 'traditional' ghosts associated with Dundee. The kind of ghosts typically trotted out when database-dependent paranormal websites and popular 'haunted' compilations briefly turn their attention to the city. Be warned, in this chapter I trust the word 'tradition' about as far as I can throw a piano.

The Tay Bridge Disaster

On the night of 28 December 1879, the Tay Railway Bridge – one of the engineering wonders of the Victorian age – collapsed, pitching the train crossing it into the waters of the storm-tossed river below. The entire complement of crew and passengers were lost, seventy-five people in total; it took weeks for some bodies to wash ashore, often miles downriver from the site. Other corpses were never recovered. In terms of the impact on Dundee and the local community, the tragedy was the railway equivalent of the sinking of the *Titanic*.

In retrospect, the bridge was an accident waiting to happen. The design of the two-mile-long structure had been based on inaccurate calculations about wind strength, having been constructed to survive force 6 gales when – as on the night in question – a storm coming down the Tay could blow force 10. A storm in February 1877 had already caused a great deal of damage, and marooned fifty-four workmen for a terrifying night out in the river. The iron used in the construction was not of top quality, and costs had been cut in other areas during the six-year construction period. While most of the brick or brick-and-iron viaduct piers were set into solid rock, one sat on shifting gravel. One of the high girders of the central span had collapsed during the construction, but was salvaged, straightened and replaced in its original position. Unfortunately, this weakened girder gradually became distorted, creating a kink in the trackbed of the rails. So, on the night of the disaster, the bridge was already in 'collapse-critical' condition. The catalyst was the train itself. As the engine, guard's brake, first-class carriage, second-class carriage and four third-class carriages passed over the kink, an exceptionally strong gust blew the last carriage against the bridge super-structure, damaging the lugs that attached the high girders to the vertical towers. With

The Tay Bridge after the disaster. (Author's collection)

The new Tay Bridge. From The Queen's Empire – A Pictorial & Descriptive Record, *1897*

the lugs and girders already overstrained by the storm, the entire central section of the bridge simply fell apart.

The bridge had also been the scene of an earlier tragedy, in August 1873, when the upper part of a cylinder – a giant structure being sunk through the river bottom to the bedrock – cracked open. Six men who were working inside the cylinder, guiding it down, all drowned.

Locomotive NBR 224, the engine from the disaster, was recovered, and worked for several more years on the railways, under the gallows-humour name of 'The Diver'. In other circumstances – say a novel by Stephen King – the drowned workmen from the disaster would give rise to stories of malevolent horrors associated with the disaster's material descendants – the 'haunted bridge' or the 'cursed locomotive'. But the main supernatural story that clings to the Tay Bridge disaster is that of an anniversary apparition.

It is said that at 7.15 p.m. on 28 December, a steam train has been seen crossing the current Tay Railway Bridge at full power, only to disappear halfway across, accompanied by the sounds of screams and screeching metal. In this, the Tay Bridge joins a select group of British sites folklorically associated with phantom trains. Apparitional locomotives are apparently present at Soham in Cambridgeshire and Washford in Somerset, each location being the site of a fatal disaster.

Unfortunately, despite the Tay Bridge phantom train being a 'well-known' event witnessed by 'many people', it has proved impossible to track down any reliable sightings (I myself once spent an evening on the anniversary looking at the bridge; nothing crossed except ordinary ScotRail trains; it was chilly and wet, and I went home with the beginnings of a cold). Further claims that the ghost train is seen racing across the bridge are unlikely to say the least, as the standard speed for the crossing was a mere 3mph. I therefore suggest that, in the absence of any reliable eyewitness sightings, the 'ghost train' is simply an urban legend, indicative of the hold the Tay Bridge disaster still has on the city's collective imagination.

The only verifiable 'ghost' associated with the 1879 disaster is a purely fictional one. In 2010, Dundee Rep Theatre staged *The Bridge*, which featured the ghost of a victim. The play's writer, Kevin Dyer, and director, Michael Judge, were kind enough to guide me through the creation of the story, which originated in ideas generated by the Dundee Rep Community Theatre Company. Based on the real-life story of two lovers who both perished on the train, the play invents the circumstances in which the man's body was found, but the woman's body was not. What happens instead is that the corpse of Eliza Smart is dragged from the river by Muggie Shah, a derelict woman

based on a real-life Dundee drunk of the period. Shah keeps the body unburied for many years, and for this reason the spirit of the girl cannot rest. She returns to haunt the Queen's Hotel – where, fictionally, she worked before her death – and, at a wedding reception in 2010, sees a man who resembles her lost partner.

There is one intriguing preternatural coda to the 1879 disaster, which suggests – but does not prove – precognitive knowledge of the disaster in advance. In 1894, Frank Podmore, one of the founders of the Society for Psychical Research, published a work entitled *Apparitions and Thought-Transference: An Examination of the Evidence for Telepathy*. In it, he included a letter from 'Miss Y.' of Perth, in 1879. One Sunday evening, Miss Y. had been struck with a dreadful premonition:

> Suddenly an eerie feeling came over me … ideas of death and disaster haunted me so persistently. It was a vague but intense feeling; a sudden ghastly realisation of human tragedy, with no 'where', 'how', or 'when' about it.

She went and shared her feelings with her mother, who confirmed that the girl, 'suddenly came running upstairs to me, saying that she had heard shrieks in the air; that something dreadful must have happened, for the air seemed full of shrieks. She thought a great many people must be dying.'

The following morning, the household learned of the Tay Bridge disaster.

The Wishart Arch

This sixteenth-century arch has been the site of ghostly sermons, while the screams and wails of the diseased and dying have also been heard.

Supposedly.
Allegedly.
So they say.
That's the rumour.
That's what they say.
That's what I've heard.
It must be true, because the tradition exists.

Hmm…

In 1544, George Wishart, a Protestant firebrand who had already been banned from Dundee by the Catholic authorities, was back in the city administering spiritual comfort to the victims of the plague. At the time, Dundee had five gates or 'ports'

leading into the city – Cowgate, Seagate, Argyle Gate (aka Overgate Port), Wellgate Port and Westport. These were not defensive structures designed to keep enemies out; they merely acted as 'control points' where customs dues were levied on goods coming in. When the plague-stricken were removed outside the Burgh to what were called Sick-Men's Wards, Wishart famously mounted the top of one of the ports so that he could preach to both the healthy inside the city and the diseased outwith the boundaries. Two years later, Wishart was burned alive by order of Cardinal Beaton at St Andrews, thus becoming one of the most significant martyrs of the Scottish Reformation.

Of all the city's ports, the one now called the Wishart Arch is the only example to have survived, the council having resisted many calls for its demolition (as early as 1833, complaints were lodged about the narrowness of the arch, which prevented the passage

The Wishart Arch when it used to span Cowgate. (Author's collection)

The Wishart Arch today. (The Author)

of carts and carriages down Cowgate). After being damaged by vehicle strikes in the 1970s and '80s, the road was closed. Following subsequent redevelopment, the ancient structure no longer blocks the road it once controlled, and stands isolated on the part of Cowgate to the east of the East Marketgait, the inner ring road that now bisects the once-historic thoroughfare.

Sadly, nothing about the ghost story stands up to scrutiny. Firstly, archaeological enquiry has shown that George Wishart could not have preached from the so-called Wishart Arch. The structure was actually built in 1591, almost half a century after the preacher's famous actions. The arch that Wishart preached from stood on Seagate, not Cowgate, and, like the other ports, was demolished in the late eighteenth century. As for the alleged sounds, there is not a single recorded witness statement. Generations of Dundee children have been taught about

the Wishart Arch, and I have no doubt that its local fame has generated the tradition.

Claypotts Castle

> There are many absurd traditions regarding Claypotts Castle afloat in the locality, which will not bear examination.

A.H. Millar, *The Historical Castles and Mansions of Scotland – Perthshire and Forfarshire*

A.H. Millar was Dundee's chief librarian and a prolific author of books on the history of his city. The 'absurd traditions' that he refers to, with regards to this castle, come down to two ghost stories: the lady who forlornly waves her white handkerchief from the battlements in the vain hope that her lover will come; and horrid screams and red glows associated with the Satanic dabbling of a great Jacobite hero. Sadly, neither of these tales has any substance to them, although they do offer an insight into the way complex historical events and famous figures are distilled into folklore and romanticised ghost stories. Not everyone can get excited about the details of the Scottish Reformation or the political struggles between two seventeenth-century dynasties, but lost love and dastardly ambition are personal stories that never go out of fashion.

Claypotts Castle. Ghostly White Lady and Satanic red glow not shown! (The Author)

The 'White Lady', who supposedly signals from the battlements on 29 May each year, is identified as Marion Ogilvy, the life partner of Cardinal David Beaton, Archbishop of St Andrews. Beaton was a key figure in the resistance of Catholic Scotland against the forthcoming Protestant Reformation (it was he who had executed George Wishart as a heretic). He was rich, powerful and brilliant. Ogilvy and the cardinal were together for more than two decades, and had eight children – but, because of his religious position, the couple could not get married. Their relationship was characterised by the then-common (at least for senior churchmen) status of concubinage. As a concubine, Ogilvy had legal rights and all the couple's children were fully recognised in law, and each inherited estates and castles. Ogilvy herself was a formidable businesswoman who managed her own affairs, and was often found in the Edinburgh courts suing for one thing or another.

The conventional story goes that Beaton built Claypotts Castle as a residence for his beloved, and when Ogilvy fancied a bit of company, she would ascend to the parapet and wave her white handkerchief. This signal would be picked up by a lookout at St Andrew's Castle, and the cardinal would then ride out, cross the Tay by ferry, and meet up with his paramour at Claypotts. On 29 May 1546, she performed the handkerchief waving as usual, but her lover did not respond – because he had just been brutally assassinated at St Andrews by Protestant conspirators. Each year on 29 May, Marion Ogilvy stands on the upper walkway of Claypotts Castle, waving her white handkerchief for a man who will never come.

You can see the romantic appeal of this particular ghost story. It has the right ingredients – tragic lost love and famous people from Scotland's turbulent past. It is also a load of hooey. Let's start with the historical farrago.

Firstly, Claypotts Castle was only started in 1569, some twenty-three years after the cardinal's death. Neither he nor Ogilvy owned any of the land around it, and Marion never lived there. She spent much of her time at Ethie Castle near Arbroath, and lived at Melgund Castle near Aberlemno until her death in 1575.

Secondly, it is utterly absurd to think that a signal from Claypotts can be seen in St Andrews, some 13 miles away, across an estuary and the undulating land of East Fife. The story may be a corrupted version of another tradition, that when Cardinal Beaton was due to cross the Tay, flags were raised at the castles of Tayport and Dundee (both castles have long since vanished).

One of the interior rooms in Claypotts. (The Author)

Thirdly, Marion Ogilvy was not waiting for Beaton on 29 May 1546 – she was at St Andrews with him. As is made clear in Margaret Sanderson's superbly detailed biography of Beaton, *Cardinal of Scotland*, the conspirators saw her leave the postern gate just before they forced themselves into St Andrew's Castle.

The predominantly Protestant historians of the nineteenth century gave Beaton's reputation a good drubbing, taking his relationship with Marion Ogilvy as evidence of clerical licentiousness, and ascribing to him an entirely unjustified and non-existent series of mistresses (the castles he was supposed to have gifted to his many lovers were in fact designed to accommodate his four daughters). For a long time Beaton was castigated more for being a sexual being – who in truth had just one partner – than for burning Protestants. Possibly propelled by this undue emphasis on the cardinal's love life, Claypotts became the setting for a spurious episode of a glamorous Renaissance romance.

But why is Claypotts supposedly haunted by Marion Ogilvy and not Melgund or Ethie? (According to William Marshall's book *Historic Scenes in Forfarshire*, Beaton still haunts Ethie Castle.) This is a harder nut to crack. Perhaps it is related to the location and history of the castle. As Dundee and Broughty Ferry expanded in the nineteenth century, many urban dwellers passing on the main road between the two would have become familiar with the strikingly tall and ancient building – so different to city dwellings and exactly the kind of place to attract 'castle legends'. Around the same time, Claypotts went downmarket, becoming a residence for farm labourers. It is feasible that working men living in such a grand setting would tell stories about the place being haunted.

The reliable Joseph Lee references this period in his poem 'The White

Lady of Claypotts Castle (or The Night's Adventures of Jock Kinmond, Ploughman)' another episode in his 1910 collection, *Poems: Tales o' Our Town*. Jock Kinmond leaves his lady-love late at night and strolls back to his home at Claypotts. Already spooked by an owl's call he mistook for a scream, Jock encounters a greater horror as he approaches the castle:

> And then his blood chills down to zero,
> For there, as imitating Hero,
> The White Ladye waves from the wa'
> And to the sea looks out in sorrow,
> As she her lover back would ca'
> Perchance he cometh on the morrow?
> Jock waits nae mair, but wi' a roar,
> Bangs breathless through the bothy door.

He relates his terrifying adventure to his fellow ploughman Dave, who, instead of sympathising, laughs at the young man, because Jock has made the classic mistake of instantly ascribing his experience to the supernatural, without considering other more mundane possibilities. In Lee's rationalist take on the episode, the 'ghost' is a piece of laundry:

> Dave could contain himself nae langer,
> Tho' unco sweer to spoil the sport,
> And mair in anguish than in anger,
> Cried, "Jock, ye muckle moudiwort!
> What ye saw wavin' in the dark,
> Was my new-scoured white Sunday sark!"

It is possible, of course, that the White Lady of Claypotts is genuine, and that it is only her identification with Marion Ogilvy that is inauthentic. In which case, we should discard the Ogilvy/Beaton mythology and concentrate solely on the reported sightings of the ghost. But, sadly, there are no such sightings that I can find. Everyone knows about the spectre at Claypotts, but no one seems to have actually written down anything about her being spotted.

In general, Claypotts Castle is closed to the public and one must settle for an exterior view; however, the interior can be visited by prior arrangement with Historic Scotland (the details are at the end of this book). With a Z-plan fortified domestic tower house, consisting of a central block and two flanking towers, the sixteenth-century castle was never attacked and never even lost its roof. It is in superb condition, with many original features still remaining. The present caretaker, Murdo Wilson, who has been in place for fifteen years, has never had a single sighting of the White Lady, nor indeed of the castle's other, supposed haunting – the spectral fires and screams resulting from Satanic worship.

Although Claypotts was built by the locally prominent Strachan family, by the early seventeenth century it had passed to the more powerful Grahams, a lowland clan. This clan had many prominent members, like the Marquis of Montrose, who led a rebellion during the Civil Wars, and they often had a huge impact on Scottish history. Later in the century, the owner was John Graham of Claverhouse, Viscount Dundee. Although he spent very little time at Claypotts, and never lived there, Claverhouse's fame – or infamy, depending on your point of view – is the starting point for the story of the haunting.

Claverhouse, one of the most brilliant generals of his time, had been a loyal supporter of the Stuart kings' attempt to suppress religious dissent in Scotland, and had mercilessly harried the ultra-Protestant rebels known as the Covenanters. This persecution, combined with his leadership qualities, personal charisma and superb tactical ability (he only lost one battle, and that was early on in his career) garnered him an unusual reputation. His enemies spread the rumour that 'Bonnie Dundee' had sold his soul to the Devil. In exchange, Claverhouse was made invulnerable to sword and shot (he indeed sailed through the thick of fighting unscathed, but that was more down to his personal courage and skill). Further, the Devil supplied the general with a black charger taken from Hell's own stables.

By the time Claverhouse declared for the exiled James II and the Jacobite rebels in 1688, both his military prowess and the rumours about him were at their height. The following year, he scored a decisive victory over a Government army at the Battle of Killiecrankie in Highland Perthshire, a textbook example of a smaller force using battlefield tactics and the advantage of terrain to defeat a much larger opponent. But as the battle came to its close, Claverhouse was shot and, Nelson-like, expired at the moment of his greatest victory. Within days, the word was that he had been killed not by a normal round, but by a silver bullet. Even more supernatural legends gathered around him – the night before he died, he was said to have had a vengeful vision of a Covenanter he had killed, and at the moment of his death his spirit was supposed to have appeared to a friend many miles away.

Claverhouse – and his capital 'R' Romantic life and death – joined the list of Scottish heroes whose legend became widespread, especially in the nineteenth century when Jacobite romanticism was at its height. In Dundee, this seems to have prompted the following train of thought:

Claverhouse sold his soul to Satan + Claverhouse owned Claypotts = Claverhouse must have sold his soul at Claypotts

From such unassailable logic, Claypotts became regarded as the locus of stereotyped, even clichéd, events at Hallowe'en: the castle ringing with the laughter and shrieks of witchcraft orgies, while the glow of infernal fires heralded Satan's continuing influence. But, folkloric imaginings aside, did anyone ever actually witness such demonic cantrips at Claypotts? In a word, no. There are no records. No sightings. No red glow. No sounds of witches partying. Just another myth born of the popular versions of Scottish history.

One of the peculiarities of the story is that Claverhouse's Faustian pact is associated with a property that he barely visited. He spent most of his early life resident at Glen Ogilvie near Glamis, and in 1683 acquired the more substantial Dudhope Castle as his principal home. Dudhope, now part of the University of Abertay, is still there, sitting imposingly on an escarpment north of Lochee Road. Yet, despite its obvious age and bulk, there is not a whiff of brimstone associated with the place, while Claypotts is Satan central.

Popular Rhymes of Scotland, a compilation of balladry, verse and folklore published by Robert Chambers in 1841, includes the story of the Brownie of Claypotts Castle. Brownies were staple fixtures in British folklore, being diminutive supernatural beings who helped out in kitchens and farms, in exchange for only the simplest of creature comforts. Brownies almost always suffered from Obsessive-Compulsive Cleaning Disorder. One day, when a maid carelessly and messily prepared vegetables, the Brownie flew into a rage, beat the poor girl with the discarded stalks, and quit the castle in a huff. Compared to Marion Ogilvy's ghostly handkerchief and Claverhouse's hellish haunting, the Brownie seems relatively plausible.

The Black Lady of Logie

The Black Lady was supposedly an Indian princess whose mournful spirit flitted around Logie House, on the road between Dundee and Lochee. By the early part of the nineteenth century, she was Dundee's most famous ghost, and her tragic story featured in both local folklore and several works of true-story type fiction.

All of which is mightily strange, as the lady in question almost certainly did not exist, and Fletcher Read, the alleged villain of the piece, was entirely innocent of the calumny posthumously claimed against him. This particular folk ghost is an abject lesson in the way real personal histories and the presence of a spooky building can be twisted together and distorted into a completely unwarranted supernatural tale – and as such, it is a tutorial for more modern cases of ghost-hunting and paranormal belief.

Until just over 100 years ago, Logie House stood at the spot that is now Black Street, an open public space bounded by Mitchell Street, Benvie Street, Cleghorn Street and Lochee Road. Its inclusion within the infrastructure of the city forms the first clue in the development of the ghost story, for here we have a grand mansion in full view of a poor working population living in urban squalor – inevitably, stories would be told about the 'big house'.

The building of Logie House was started in 1722. In 1797, Fletcher Read of Cairnie, the supposed villain of the tale, inherited the property. He was known locally for his tendency to spend the family's cash on gambling, drinking and high-living. In his youth, he and several other young gentlemen of rank, including William Ramsay (Baron Panmure), had been involved in a notorious drunken episode. They

The now-demolished Logie House is the mansion in the trees. The 'Cradle' would have been somewhere nearby. (Local History Library, Leisure & Culture Dundee)

had dressed in white sheets and invaded Logie Cemetery (a quarter of a mile from Logie House), then they blew trumpets over the graves, as a mockery of the Last Resurrection and Judgement. It was perhaps this much-exaggerated episode, combined with his well-known appetite for dissipation, that saw Fletcher Read cast as the black-hearted bad guy of the Black Lady tale. The basic story, as known from the early nineteenth century, and with several variants thereafter, claims that the laird went to India as part of the East India Company. There he wooed the beautiful daughter of a prince or Maharajah, and, on marrying her, he was placed in charge of a fabulous dowry of gold and jewels. In return, he told his father-in-law that he would care for his new bride as does a mother 'looking after her child in a cradle'. Back in Dundee, he abandoned his exotic bride and had her imprisoned in a specially built structure in the grounds of Logie House which he

cynically referred to as the Cradle, for as such he was fulfilling his promise to her father. And here, attended only by an aged female servant or ayah, the Indian princess declined away, and eventually died. Fletcher Read was lured back to India, where the girl's father had him torn apart by a galloping horse attached to each limb.

This is all very gruesome and Gothic; and all entirely nonsense.

Fletcher Read was never on the subcontinent and was never an officer in the East India Company. He was legally married to Jean Scott, and there is no further indication of any other wife, Indian or otherwise. And he most certainly did not die by being torn apart by four horses. In fact, his death was, given his drinking habits, boringly predictable. The *Scots Magazine* for 1807 records his departure from this life:

At Shepperton, Surrey, January 22, Fletcher Read, a gentleman well known in the sporting world. He had spent the previous evening with some convivial friends, and was found dead in his bed on the ensuing morning by his servant, having, it is supposed, died through suffocation.

'Died through suffocation' here is almost certainly a code for 'choked on his own vomit'.

The tale may have originated because two of Fletcher Read's uncles, Thomas and Robert Fletcher, spent many years in India. But again, there is no record of either of them having an Indian wife. We are on much stronger ground when it comes to the so-called Cradle, which definitely did exist. The *Courier's* pseudonymous roving correspondent, S.S., published another one of his series 'Wanderings about the Antique Places & Churchyards of Forfarshire and Borders of Perthshire, &c.', on 6 December 1848:

> In the year 1812, a few yards beyond Logie farm was to be seen a dull unsheltered disagreeable looking house of two stories. This house from having a pavilion formed roof and a short chimney stalk of two flues perched on the top of each of its four corners, was familiarly known as the 'Cradle House', from some fancied resemblance it bore to that useful piece of family furniture.

In his 1909 book, *Dundee Past and Present*, William Kidd published the reminiscences of Lochee-based Mrs Home Scott, born Mary Jobson in 1797, who died as an elderly woman in 1879. 'At the top of Logie Strip,' she recounted, 'a building stood that contained the "Cradle", and no one liked to approach it as it was said to be haunted.'

From the description of a 'pavilion formed roof' and its position in the grounds of Logie House, it is clear that this was a summerhouse, probably with an architectural style derived from an Asian original. This was a common kind of construction in the late eighteenth century, when old India hands retired to Britain and erected pleasure houses in their gardens to remind them of hot, sunny days. Unfortunately, no one sketched the summerhouse, and so we can only guess how it really looked. But a summerhouse in full view of the road was hardly going to make an effective gaol, and I think we can dismiss the 'Cradle' as being the prison of an abandoned and incarcerated woman.

I therefore speculate that several factors came together to create the legend of the Black Lady of Logie: the location of grand Logie House in an increasingly urban area; the view of the unusual summerhouse from the road; the wastrel habits of Fletcher Read; and the Indian connections of his uncles. Add to this the likely confusion over names in the prolific Read/Fletcher family histories, combined with the kinds of stories the poor and downtrodden tend to tell about the rich and powerful, and you have a rich stew of what, in the technical language of folklore, is known as 'making things up as you go along'.

As for the ghost, there is little to say, as in narrative terms she is merely a function of the bigger story of aristocratic cruelty, and justified in bloody revenge. A post-modern reading may see her as a symbol of the unequal and fractious relationship between Dundee and its flax-suppliers in India. There are absolutely no recorded sightings of the phantom. Despite 200 years of her tale being told, the Black Lady of Logie is nothing more than a ghost of Gothic romance, a spirit of storytelling.

Bell Street car park

This is a relatively modern tradition – the notion that ghostly cries and sobs are heard near the multi-storey car park between Bell Street and Marketgait, on account of the fact that the site was built on a cemetery. Yes, it's another Stephen King moment.

The Constitution Road Cemetery opened for business in 1836, being designed to take the pressure off the grotesquely overcrowded Howff boneyard a few streets to the south. On 17 January 1840, the body of small child was found hidden on the north border of the graveyard. Such incidents were not uncommon in industrial Britain, where high infant mortality and inflated burial fees caused many working-class families to dispose of their dead, especially their dead babies, secretly. The new cemetery quickly filled up and was closed to new interments in 1882, although lair-holders could still have memorials set up for relatives who were buried elsewhere. The entire site was cleared in 1962 – except for five headstones which still remain attached to the former west wall of the graveyard, and can be found alongside the footpath on the north-western corner of the car park.

I wonder if the incongruous sight of a row of Victorian gravestones, next to a modern multi-storey car park, is the root of the alleged reports that the dead are heard wailing near here. If no memorials had remained, would the stories have been generated? Of the inscriptions, one commemorates William Brown, flax spinner; another two are memorials to various members of the Walker and Neish families; and the others record the passing of David, the infant son of David Small, and the deaths of Patrick Watson and Margaret Low, plus their five children. The latter include Euphemia, who was eight when she died, Andrew Low (three), Jessie (nine months) and Christina (one month). The Small and Watson/Low children are of interest because the most persistent description of the sounds is that of a child crying. Could someone have read the inscriptions, been moved by the appallingly young age of the children at the time of their deaths, and then started the ball rolling, folklorically speaking?

On the other hand (that phrase again), perhaps there is something to the stories. A few years ago, Tom Rannachan, author of *Psychic Scotland*, received an email from a female witness who said she had been getting into her car one afternoon when she felt a little invisible hand grabbing hers, followed by the sound of a child crying. She searched the deserted car park for a few moments and then, thoroughly spooked, jumped back into the car and drove off.

On the left, Bell Street multi-storey car park. On the right, the last gravestones from the Constitution Road Cemetery. (The Author)

eight

Historic Hauntings

THE people of Dundee have been interested in ghosts for a long time. In 1587, the rich and intellectually inclined merchant David Wedderburne owned a book entitled *Of Ghostes and Spirites Walking by Night, and of Strange Noyses, Crackes and Sundrie Forewarnynges*, written by Lewes Lauaterus, or Lavater, in 1572. Lavater argued that many ghost sightings were the result of hallucinations and hoaxes, and that the few that were genuine were not the spirits of the dead, but demons in disguise.

The Eighteenth Century

The earliest recorded ghost report from Dundee dates from the year 1708, or thereabouts. The witness was the Revd James Mercer of Clevage. Mercer had been born around 1686, graduating from St Andrews twenty years later, when he was described as both academically gifted and 'a young man who has been well and piously inclined, and hath had a very Christian conversation from his youth up'. In 1710, he became the minister at Forteviot in Perthshire, being promoted to the neighbouring parish of Aberdalgie and Dupplin eight years later,

at the behest of his friend and patron, Thomas, the 6th Earl of Kinnoull. In other words, as both a stalwart of the Presbyterian Church, and the friend of an aristocrat, he was through and through a 'solid' member of the Establishment. (More background about the Revd Mercer can be found in *Dunning: Its Parochial History*, by John Wilson.)

Some time before he was 'called' to Forteviot, Mr Mercer stayed in a set of rooms in Dundee. His landlady was the widow of Dundee skipper Captain William Bell, whose death had brought her to reduced circumstances. In 1710, as Hamish Robertson's *Mariners of Dundee* notes, she started a court action under her maiden name of Barbara Taylor, looking to reclaim one-eighth of the profit deriving from her husband's ship *Margaret* for the years 1703-4. Mercer described her as 'a very good woman', and clearly sympathised with her financial plight.

James Mercer had been staying in one of Mrs Bell's rooms for a short while, when he heard the room door open just as he went to bed. He assumed it was a servant looking to remove his shoes for cleaning, but, on enquiring the next day, he found this

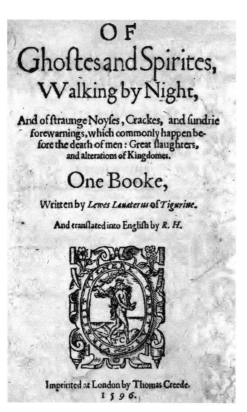

OF
Ghoſtes and Spirites,
Walking by Night,

And of ſtraunge Noyſes, Crackes, and ſundrie
forewarnings, which commonly happen before the death of men : Great ſlaughters,
and alterations of Kingdomes.

One Booke,

Written by *Lewes Lauaterus* of *Tigurine*.

And tranſlated into Engliſh by *R. H.*

Imprinted at London by Thomas Creede.
1 5 9 6.

Of Ghostes and Spirites Walking by Night – *the 1596 edition.*

was not the case. His landlady stated that the servants had talked of seeing apparitions, but that such things were harmless, and she hoped the fine young gentleman would not be scared away. The next night the door swung open again, and within the frame Mercer saw 'two boys, in sea-men's habits, standing and looking into the room'. The following night the same thing happened, only this time the two figures advanced a little into the room. The episode was repeated night after night, with the boys coming closer each time. Finally, on the fourteenth night, they came right to Mercer's bedside, and then disappeared. Not once had the apparitions spoken, and Mercer himself had resolved not to address the spirits directly.

It did not take long to discover the alleged identity of the apparitions. Captain

Bell had taken two poor Dundonian lads to America, pretending to employ them as servants. In fact, he had sold them into indentured servitude, a form of slavery (this was a common practice at the time – many of the 'lower orders' of Aberdeen, for example, were kidnapped and transported to virtual slavery in colonial America, making a handsome profit for both kidnappers and ship owners). William Bell, however, had died overseas; it was presumed that the two boys had also perished – or been murdered – and were now returning to haunt the house of their abductor's widow.

Mr Mercer was now in a quandary. Mrs Bell's establishment suited him very well (which presumably meant that it was both clean and cheap); and he knew that if he left he would not only deprive her of an income, but that gossip would follow, and the house's reputation might suffer. The spirits had not scared or harmed him, so on balance he decided to stay and not mention the incidents. And after the two boys vanished, he was troubled no more.

As with many antique apparitions, it is difficult to adequately interrogate the episode, simply because we have so little detail. The haunting was written up by the Revd Robert Wodrow (1679-1734), Minister of Eastwood in Glasgow and an assiduous, if slightly obsessive, historian of the Church of Scotland. Wodrow had heard the story not from Mercer directly, but second-hand through an intermediary, a Mr William Brown. Woodrow noted it down in what became his *Analecta*, a gossipy hodgepodge of personal journal, political news, infelicities at Court, antiquarianism, personal correspondence, Church scandal – and supernaturalism. Wodrow, in fact, like several other Presbyterian ministers, was a keen collector of paranormal experiences, from visions and precognitive dreams to Acts of

God, omens, second sight and encounters with supernatural entities, including ghosts. He has often been criticised for being overly credulous; but, on the other hand, he never had a personal paranormal experience himself, and makes it clear that he is not vouching for the authenticity of the various reports, merely being the person who is jotting the details down as he heard them. So, in terms of what actually happened, we have to assume that the Revd Mercer accurately described the episodes many years after they happened, and that William Brown did not add or subtract anything when later relating the story to Wodrow. As to where Mercer's apparitions were seen, we can but guess. The records are silent as to Mrs Bell's address, and the overwhelming majority of Dundee's medieval and post-medieval buildings have long since been swept away by destruction, decay and development.

By and large, the remainder of the eighteenth century was a quiet one for the ghosts of Dundee, and, indeed, by 1799 at least one Dundonian writer was bemoaning the state of paranormal affairs in his city. Signing his name 'Philetas' in the *Dundee Magazine*, he wrote:

> We tread not now on fairy ground. Spirits and hobgoblins are little known in these days; they flee from society and refinement, and from the busy haunts of men. These incorporeals are suffered to glide and betake themselves to cloisters, churchyards, and dormitories, and to melancholy aisles. As rooks, magpies and foxes, they nestle and burrow in the deserted and mouldering tower, and ancient chateau; and there they caw and howl to the midnight wind. 'Tis there only they hold their frantic orgies, take their nocturnal rambles, and startle the

watchful and lonely sentinel at his post. 'Tis there, mayhap, the ghosts of Malcolm and Claverhouse perambulate a dreary scene, perform their antic rounds – and vanish in the morning air!

The Nineteenth Century

The first spectre of the century, headlined under the title 'A GHOST IN LOCHEE', comes in the *Advertiser* for 29 September 1831. An elderly couple had had many of their nights disturbed by a noisy presence between midnight and 3 a.m. 'The unhallowed presence is announced by a loud battering,' the paper reported, 'which subsides for a little, and again commences with redoubled fury.' Things got so bad that the wife applied to the Lochee Kirk Session for an exorcism; Presbyterians being less inclined to exorcise manifest evil than Catholics, the request was turned down. So the neighbours were called in, and we are told that 'fourteen individuals stationed themselves within and around the house'. Unfortunately, nothing was discovered, although no details were supplied as to whether the noises were heard during this vigil. The brief article finished with the enticing sign-off: 'Vigorous measures are about to be adopted for the dislodgement of the intruder; and the probability of success is affording ample matter for speculation.'

But sadly – and typically – that is that. There was no follow-up article, and so we are left to guess just what these 'vigorous measures' were, and whether or not they were successful. No names or addresses are given, no witnesses are quoted, and even the noises themselves are barely described. Was it a poltergeist? A hoax? It is impossible to tell. It is clear that the phenomena were exclusively aural, and that no apparition was seen. Other than that, we are entirely in the dark about this particular Lochee ghost.

The next episode, found in the *Courier* on 3 July 1872 under the headline 'EXTRAORDINARY GHOST STORY IN DUNDEE', is a kind of supernatural soap opera. A woman left her husband and five children to go and live with a 'sprightly young gardener' in Dundee. When she contracted smallpox, she made her lover promise that he would seek custody of her two youngest children. Several weeks after she died, the young man had still done nothing about his promise, and one night was visited by the woman's angry spirit. The gardener was given a fortnight's grace, but if he had not fulfilled his oath by then, she told him that Death would come for him. Terrified, he approached the father of the children, who dismissed the request out of hand. Over the next two weeks the gardener became more and more desperate, being unable to sleep for fear of his fate.

The paper took up the story:

> At length the looked for and dreaded time arrived, and on Friday evening last, as he was lighting his fire previous to the evening meal, a hand was laid forcibly on his shoulder, and a sepulchral tone exclaimed, 'William, why have you not got my children? You coward, go and have them by this day week, else you die.'

The poor wretch was chained to the spot, and lay for some hours insensible. At length, when he came to himself, he ran to the house of a friend, and told the whole affair, which seemed to give him some relief. Ever since, he has refused to go into the house, and 'thoroughly believes the apparition to have been real'.

No one is named, of course – the scandal would be too great – and the tone of the article cleverly manages to avoid both scepticism and credulity, making no suggestion that the young man was either deluded or genuinely troubled by a spirit. Is the episode 'true'? A joke? A fantasy? From the text it is hard to tell. The narrative of a promise-breaker haunted by a vengeful spirit is a common element in dozens of folk tales, and so it may seem to be a piece of folklore masquerading as journalistic fact. On the other hand, such moral narratives usually have a 'pay-off' – either the faithless miscreant finally fulfils his promise just before the denizens of the dark regions come for him, or he fails to do so and is embraced by one of the many manifestations of Death or the Devil. In this case, however, the gardener has not yet reached the end of his story, for a few days have to pass before the deadline, and so we the readers are denied the expected conclusion. And we are permanently cheated, because there was no follow-up story, so we never learn what happened to the haunted gardener. Is this because the entire story was invented? Or that nothing further happened? Sadly, we shall probably never know.

Two Dundee Doubles

We conclude this book with two of the most extraordinary paranormal events yet encountered – a pair of episodes from the late Victorian era that feature the doubles of people apparently projected forward in space and time. Doubles are often termed doppelgängers, but strictly this refers to a double that is seen at the same time and place as the source; doubles seen in advance of a person's appearance are called fetches. The two fetches were described by Robert Kidd, of Gray Street, Broughty Ferry, a former police commissioner and magistrate of Dundee, and published in *Real Ghost Stories* by William T. Stead in 1891/92. Here is Mr Kidd's own experience:

A few years ago I had a shop on the High Street of Dundee – one door and one window, a cellar underneath, the entrance to which was at one corner of the shop. There was no way of getting in or out of the cellar but by that stair in the corner. It was lighted from the street by glass, but to protect that there was an iron grating, which was fixed down. Well, I had an old man, a servant, named Robert Chester. I sent him a message one forenoon about 12 o'clock; he was in no hurry returning. I remarked to my daughter, who was a book-keeper, whose desk was just by the trap-door, that he was stopping long. Just as I spoke he passed the window, came in at the door, carrying a large dish under his arm, went right past me, past my daughter, who looked at him, and went down into the cellar. After a few minutes, as I heard no noise, I wondered what he could be about, and went down to see. There was no Robert there. I cannot tell what my sensations were when I realized this; there was no possibility of his getting out, and we both of us saw and heard him go down. Well, in about twenty minutes he re-passed the window, crossed the floor, and went downstairs, exactly as he had the first time. There was no hallucination on our part. My daughter is a clever, highly-gifted woman; I am seventy-eight years of age, and have seen a great deal of the world, a great reader, etc., etc., and not easily deceived or apt to be led away by fancy, and I can declare that his first appearance to us was a reality as much as the second. We concluded, and so did all his relations, that it portended his death, but he is still alive, over eighty years of age.

I give this just as it occurred, without any varnish or exaggeration whatever.

Kidd went on to describe a second episode that he was not present at himself, but which 'was much talked about at the time', and where, he assured Stead, he had interviewed all the main witnesses. This fetch was similar to the previous one, in that it was an exact, solid-looking duplicate of an employee who was running late. It did not speak, it replicated the movements the real person would make some time later, and it was observed by several witnesses. Here are Kidd's words:

Mr Alexander Drummond was a painter, who had a big business and a large staff of men. His clerk was Walter Souter, his brother-in-law, whose business it was to be at the shop (in Northgate) sharp at six o'clock in the morning, to take an account of where the men were going, quantity of material, etc. In this he was assisted by Miss Drummond. One morning he did not turn up at the hour, but at twenty past six he came in at the door and appeared very much excited; but instead of stepping to the desk, where Mr and Miss Drummond were awaiting him, he went right through the front shop and out at a side door. This in sight of Mr and Miss Drummond, and also in sight of a whole squad of workmen. Well, exactly in another twenty minutes he came in, also very much excited, and explained that it was twenty minutes past six when he awakened, and that he had run all the way from his house (he lived a mile from the place of business). He was a very exemplary, punctual man, and when Mr Drummond asked him where he went to when he came first, he was dumbfounded, and could not comprehend what was meant. To test his truthfulness, Mr Drummond went out to Walters' wife that afternoon, when she told him the same story; that it was twenty past six o'clock when he awoke, and that he was very much excited about it, as it was the first time he had slept in.

Perhaps – and it's a big perhaps – some people under stress are unwittingly able to project facsimiles of themselves a short period into the future. Or perhaps the fetches were not mental projections, but some form of glitch in the normal running of the space-time universe. Currently, the mechanism involved is beyond our understanding. But, if both reports are authentic, then clearly the fetches, although sharing the characteristics of apparitions, were certainly not the spirits of the dead. Cases like this have significant implications on the interpretation of paranormal events as merely being visitations from the dead. And they confirm my opinion that the most paranormal object in the universe is the thing we all have in common – the human brain.

Bibliography

BOOK & JOURNALS

Adams, N., *Haunted Scotland* (Mainstream Publishing, 1998)

Apted, M.A., 'The Lands and Tower of Claypotts' in *Proceedings of the Society of Antiquaries of Scotland, Volume 88 1954-56*

Barrington, M., *Grahame of Claverhouse Viscount Dundee* (Martin Secker, 1911)

Beatts, J.M., *The Municipal History of the Royal Burgh of Dundee* (J.M. Beatts, 1873)

Beatts, J.M., *Reminiscences of an Old Dundonian* (George Petrie, 1882)

Bradford, A. & D. Taylor, *Haunted Holidays* (Hunt End Books, 2002)

Buchanan, G., *The History of Scotland: From the Earliest Accounts of that Nation to the Reign of King James VI, Volume I* (James Kay, 1821)

Carrie, J., *Ancient Things in Angus* (Thomas Buncle, 1881)

Chambers, R., *Popular Rhymes of Scotland* (W. & R. Chambers, 1841)

Colville, A., *Dundee Delineated; or, A History and Description of that Town, its Institutions, Manufactures and commerce* (A. Colville & A.M. Sandeman, 1822)

Cumming, G., *Forfarshire Illustrated: Being Views of Gentlemen's Seats, Antiquities, and Scenery in Forfarshire, with Descriptive and Historical Notices* (Gershom Cumming, 1843)

Dalgetty, A.B., *The Church and Parish of Liff* (Harley & Cox, 1940)

Dash, M., 'Spring-Heeled Jack – To Victorian Bugaboo From Suburban Ghost' in Moore, S. (ed.), *Fortean Studies, Volume 3* (John Brown Publishing, 1996)

Dorward, D., *Dundee: Names, People and Places* (Mercat Press, 1998)

Dyer, K., *The Bridge* play script (2010)

Elliot, A., *Lochee as it was and as it is* (James P. Mathew & Co., 1911)

Eunson, E. & B. Early, *Old Dundee* (Stenlake Publishing, 2002)

Green, A., *Ghosts of Today* (Kaye & Ward, 1980)

Jervise, A., *The History and Traditions of the Land of the Lindsays in Angus and Mearns, with Notices of Alyth and Meigle* (David Douglas, 1882)

Jervise, A., *Memorials of Angus and The Mearns* (David Douglas, 1885)

Kay, B. (ed), *The Dundee Book: An Anthology of Living in the City* (Mainstream Publishing, 1990)

Kidd, W., *Dundee Past and Present* (William Kidd & Sons, 1909)

Lamb, A.C., *Dundee: Its Quaint and Historic Buildings* (George Petrie, 1895)

Lamb, A.C. & A.H. Millar, *Annals of Dundee 1801-1840 – Extracts from the Dundee Advertiser* (Dundee, 1908)

Lamont, S., *Is Anybody There? A Personal Investigation into Psychic Phenomena* (Mainstream Publishing, 1980)

Lee, J., *Poems: Tales o' Our Town* (George Montgomery, 1910)

Leighton, A., *Wilson's Tales of the Borders, and of Scotland. Historical, Traditionary, and Imaginative, Volume XXIII* (The Walter Scott Publishing Co., 1884)

Lindsay, M., *The Castles of Scotland* (Constable, 1986)

Linklater, M. & Hesketh, C., *Bonnie Dundee: John*

Graham of Claverhouse – For King and Conscience (Canongate, 1992)

Love, D., *Scottish Spectres* (Robert Hale, 2001)

McHarg, J.F., 'The Paranormal and the Recognition of Personal Distress' in *Journal of the Society of Psychical Research,* Vol. 51 No. 790, February 1982

McHarg, J.F., 'Cryptomnesic and Paranormal Personation: Two Contrasting Examples' in Roll, W.G., etc. (eds), *Research In Parapsychology 1982* (The Scarecrow Press, 1983)

McKean, C. & Walker, D., *Dundee: An Illustrated Architectural Guide* (RIAS, 1993)

McKean, C., Whatley, P. & Baxter, K., *Lost Dundee: Dundee's Lost Architectural Heritage* (Birlinn, 2008)

Mackenzie, A. *The Seen and the Unseen* (Weidenfield & Nicolson, 1987)

Marshall, W., *Historic Scenes in Forfarshire* (William Oliphant & Co., 1875)

Millar, A.H., *The Historical Castles and Mansions of Scotland – Perthshire and Forfarshire* (Alexander Gardner, 1890)

Millar, A.H., *Dundee Photographic Survey: Volume II, Buildings* (Dundee Free Library Committee, 1916)

Millar, A.H., *Traditions and Stories of Scottish Castles* (Sands & Co., 1927)

Millar, A.H. (ed), *The Compt Buik of David Wedderburne Merchant of Dundee* (Scottish History Society, 1898)

Miskell, L., Whatley, C.A. & Harris, B. (eds), *Victorian Dundee – Image and Reality* (Tuckwell Press, 2000)

Mitchell, A., *Pre-1855 Gravestone Inscriptions in Angus Volume 4: Dundee & Broughty Ferry* (Scottish Genealogy Society, 1984)

Moss, P., *Ghosts Over Britain* (Elm Tree Books, 1977)

Mudie, F. & Walker, D.M., *Mains Castle & The Grahams of Fintry* (Tay Historical Society, 1964)

Owen, D.D.R., *William the Lion 1143-1214: Kingship and Culture* (Tuckwell Press, 1997)

Peter, D. MacGregor, *The Baronage of Angus and Mearns* (Oliver & Boyd, 1856)

Podmore, F., *Apparitions and Thought-Transference: An Examination of the Evidence for Telepathy* (Walter Scott, 1894)

Rannachan, T., *Psychic Scotland* (Black & White Publishing, 2007)

RCAHMS, *Dundee on Record: Images of the Past* (RCAHMS, 1992)

Robertson, H., *Mariners of Dundee: Their City, Their River, Their Fraternity* (PDQ Print Services, 2006)

Sanderson, M., *Cardinal of Scotland: David Beaton, c.1494-1546* (John Donald, 1986)

Skinner, Revd W. Cumming, *The Baronie of Hilltowne Dundee – its Industrial, Social and Religious Life* (David Winter & Son, 1927)

Stead, W.T. (edited by Stead, E.W.), *Real Ghost Stories* (George H. Doran, 1921)

Stewart, D., *Sketches of the Character, Manners, and Present State of the Highlanders of Scotland with Details of the Military Service of the Highland Regiments* (Archibald Constable, 1825)

Stewart, W.R., *Welcome Aboard the Frigate Unicorn* (The Unicorn Preservation Society, 1982)

Taylor, J., *The Great Historic Families of Scotland* (J.S. Virtue & Co., 1887)

Thomson, J. (revised by James MacLaren), *The History of Dundee* (John Durham & Son, 1874)

Towill, E.S., 'The Black Lady of Logie' in *Scots Magazine,* May 1978

UPDATE, Autumn 1979 (Dundee District Council)

Warden, A.J., *Angus or Forfarshire: the Land and People, Descriptive and Historical,* 5 Vols (Charles Alexander & Co., 1880-85)

Watson, M., *Jute and Flax Mills in Dundee* (Hutton Press, 1990)

Watson, N., *Dundee: A Short History* (Black and White Publishing, 2006)

Wilson, J., *Dunning: Its Parochial History, with Notes, Antiquarian, Ecclesiastical, Baronial, and Miscellaneous* (D. Philips/Strathearn Herald Office, 1906)

Wodrow, R., *Analecta: Or Materials for a History of Remarkable Providences; Mostly Relating to Scotch Ministers and Christians.* 4 Vols (The Maitland Club, 1844)

NEWSPAPERS

Courier & Advertiser: 5 September 1945; 8 April 1976; 31 May 1976; 25 August 1978; 28 March 1979; 8 June 1979; 13 & 15 March 1980; 2 November 2007; 20 Aug 2009

Daily Record: 27 December 1999

Dundee Advertiser: 29 September 1831; 6 September 1837; 26 March 1852; 4 March 1853; 19 February 1883; 17 May 1911

Dundee Courier: 8 November 1848; 29 December 1852; 10 November 1865; 22 June 1869; 3 July 1872; 17 November 1873; 15 January 1875; 23 September 1879; 16 January 1883; 6 February 1883; 9 February 1883; 30 January 1885; 12 March 1886; 31 January 1891; 18 February 1893; 24 September 1894; 27 June 1898; 14 & 15 November 1898; 6 December 1900

Scotsman: 21 March 1846; 10 November 1882; 19 February 1883; 15 May 1883; 17 May 1911; 30 & 31 January 1935; 2 February 1935

Sun: 14 November 2008

Weekly News: 19 May 1883

WEBSITES

www.conventiondundeeandangus.co.uk
www.dundeecity.gov.uk
www.ghostfinders.co.uk
www.ghost-story.co.uk/yourstories
www.paranormaldiscovery.co.uk
www.philological.bham.ac.uk
www.scotlandsplaces.gov.uk
www.tayside.police.uk
www.youngscot.org/dundee

Index

Antarctica 23, 55-56, 58, 59
Arbroath 43, 79
Balgay Bridge & Park 11-16, 19, 21
Barnhill 71
Beaton, Cardinal David 77, 79-81
Benvie 26-27
Black Lady of Logie 83-85
Blackness 18-19, 67-68
Boece, Hector 50-52
Bonner, Charles 59
Botanic Gardens 30
Broughty Ferry 29, 68, 71, 80, 90
Buchanan, George 51-52
Catholicism 42, 50, 77, 79, 89
Caird Park 47, 50
Claypotts Castle 78-82, 93
Coffin Mill 17-21
Covenanters 81-82
Craigie 42, 68
Deaths, accidental 14, 18, 21
Den O' Mains 46-54
Dichty Burn 47
Doppelgangers 90-92
Dudhope Castle 82
Dundee Backpackers Hostel 38-40
Dundee Heritage Trust 19, 58
Dundee Rep Theatre 76
Dundee Royal Lunatic Asylum 41
Dundee Streets:
  Albert Street 41
  Arbroath Road 43, 63
  Bellfield Lane 67
  Bell Street 86
  Belltree Gardens 29-30
  Benvie Street 83
  Blackness Road 18, 67
  Black Street 83
  Brewery Lane 18
  Brook Street 17-18
  Cardean Street 41
  Cleghorn Street 83
  Constitution Road 86

Cowgate 77, 78
Craigie Street 68
Crescent Street 68, 70
East Marketgait 78
Ferry Road 68
Gray Street 90
Hawkhill 67
High Street 9, 38, 91
Horsewater Wynd 18
Kemback Street 68
Lochee Road 18, 64, 65, 82, 83
Lower Pleasance 17, 18
Marketgait 86
Mitchell Street 83
Morgan Street 40-41
Murraygate 63
Nethergate 71
North Wellington Street 68
Perth Road 30
Seagate 77, 78
South Ellen Street 71
Ure Street 16
West Henderson Wynd 19
Edinburgh 9, 10, 29, 32, 42, 79
Ethie Castle 79-80
Gardyne's Land 38-39
Gilchrist, Earl of Angus 50-52
Graham of Claverhouse, Viscount Dundee 81-82
Fetches 90-92
Forfar 71
Hilltown 43, 63, 68
HMS Unicorn 59-62, 93
Hoaxes 63-73, 87, 89
Howff, The 8, 86
India 10, 83-85
Invergowrie 26, 72
Jacobites 79, 82
Jaffrey, Grissel 8
Jute 10, 18, 19, 22, 30
Killiecrankie, Battle of 82
Kirriemuir 71
Lee, Joseph 10, 48-50, 53, 80-81
Liff 32, 41, 65-66

Lochee 11-16, 65, 68, 70, 83, 85, 89-90
Logie House 83-85
Logie Kirkyard 64-65
Logie Works 18
London 69
Longforgan 73
McHarg, Dr James 32-37
Mains Castle 47-54, 93
Mains Graveyard 46-49
Maryfield 48, 68
Melgund Castle 79-80
Mills 9-10, 17-25
Ogilvy, Marion 79-82
Perth/Perthshire 73, 76, 82, 87
Plague 26-27, 48, 77
Police 17-18, 22, 28, 43-44, 63, 65
Poltergeists 32, 34, 42-43
Precognition 76
Protestantism 77, 79, 80, 81
Pseudo psi-phenomena 33-36
Read, Fletcher 83-85
Reformation, The 27, 77, 79
Royal Research Ship Discovery 23, 55-61, 93
St Andrews 77, 79-80, 87
Satan/The Devil 79, 81-82
Scott, Captain Robert Falcon 55-56
Shackleton, Ernest 58-59
Society for Psychical Research 32-36, 93
South Georgia Heritage Trust 23-24
Spring-Heeled Jack 67-71
Suicides 14, 16, 48
Tay Rail Bridge Disaster 74-76
Temporal lobe epilepsy 33-35
Verdant Works 19-26
Wellgate Shopping Centre 43-44
William I, King 50-52
Wishart Arch 77-78
Wishart, George 77-79
Wodrow, Rev. Robert 88-89